1981

T. S. Eliot's Impersonal Theory of Poetry

T. S. Eliot's
Impersonal Theory of Poetry

Mowbray Allan

Lewisburg
Bucknell University Press

© 1974 by Associated University Presses, Inc.

Associated University Presses, Inc.
Cranbury, New Jersey 08512

Library of Congress Cataloging in Publication Data

Allan, Mowbray, 1934–
    T. S. Eliot's impersonal theory of poetry.

    Bibliography: p.
    1. Eliot, Thomas Stearns,1888–1965. 2. Poetry
—History and criticism. I. Title.
PS3509.L43Z585   801'.951   73–489
ISBN 0–8387–1311–4

To Sally

Contents

Preface

In "The Perfect Critic," T. S. Eliot proposed to inquire "how far criticism is 'feeling' and how far 'thought,' and what sort of 'thought' is permitted."[1] My subject is Eliot's critical thought; I shall not be concerned with his critical taste or with his judgments on specific writers except incidentally. However, in presuming to use the word *theory* of Eliot's critical thought, I might seem to be attributing to him a critical approach that he himself would not have permitted. Therefore, I make this qualification: I do not imply that Eliot's practice as a critic follows from a theory. Reviewing his critical career near the end of his life, Eliot remarked, "I am sure that my own theorizing has been epiphenomenal of my tastes."[2] This retrospective judgment corresponds exactly to the answers Eliot had returned, forty years before, to the questions above: "The true generalization is not something superposed upon an accumulation of perceptions; the perceptions do not, in a really appreciative mind, accumulate as a mass, but form themselves as a structure; and criticism is the statement in language of this structure; it is a development of sensibility."[3]

1. *The Sacred Wood*, 2nd ed. (London: Methuen, 1960), p. 7.
2. "To Criticize the Critic," *To Criticize the Critic* (New York: Farrar, Straus and Giroux, 1965), p. 20.
3. *The Sacred Wood*, p. 15.

9

10   T. S. Eliot's Impersonal Theory of Poetry

On the other hand, "The Perfect Critic" also rejects the feasibility of critical impressionism, the idea that criticism can simply "exhibit to us, like the plate, the faithful record of the impressions, more numerous or more refined than our own, upon a mind more sensitive than our own."[4] And in Eliot's early criticism, that represented by *The Sacred Wood,* we find phrases or even whole passages in a kind of metaphysical vocabulary that suggests, darkly, the presence of an underlying theory. That this theory remained largely esoteric is due, I think, to a deliberate decision on Eliot's part. He wrote in 1917, "The essential is, that our philosophy should spring from our point of view and not return upon itself to explain our point of view."[5] However, I believe that it is possible, by beginning with Eliot's thesis on F. H. Bradley, to arrive at an understanding of the metaphysical vocabulary referred to.

This essay takes the form of analyses of the fundamental terms in Eliot's critical vocabulary: Point of View, Thought and Sensation, Self-consciousness, Object, Personality, Form. And I take my turn at explicating the famous phrases "objective correlative" and "dissociation of sensibility." But I also mean to reveal the pattern of relationships among these terms. This pattern is tightly knit indeed. For example, Eliot's attitude to personality, his theory of the dissociation of sensibility, and his sociological thought are all closely and intelligibly connected. If I have hesitated to use the word *theory* of Eliot's critical thought, it is certainly *not* because it falls short in unity and coherence. The fundamental unity of Eliot's thought is, I believe, accurately reflected in the organization of my essay, which is thus at least as important as the content of the individual chapters.

I do not wish, however, to contradict Eliot's own statement of the relation of his critical practice to theory. For,

4. *Ibid.,* p. 3.
5. "Eeldrop and Appleplex, I," *The Little Review* 4 (May 1917): 10.

even if we find the elements of a reasonably complete and consistent theory in Eliot's thesis and in his early criticism, we should still have to make a distinction analogous to that which Eliot made between Dante and Goethe on the one hand and Donne on the other: "In philosophical poetry the poet believes in some theory about life and the universe and makes poetry of it. Metaphysical poetry, on the other hand, does not imply belief: it has come to mean poetry in which the poet makes use of metaphysical ideas and theories."[6] If we apply this distinction to criticism, we should have to place Eliot in the latter class. We shall find that much of Eliot's critical thought was derived from the idealist theory of knowledge, but we need not conclude from this fact that Eliot believed all the basic assumptions of the idealist theory.

I take this opportunity to thank Professors Reuben Brower and William Alfred of Harvard University, not least for their patience in reading a first draft that deserved too well the name *essay*. If I have succeeded at all in reducing to lucidity so difficult a work as Eliot's thesis, much of the credit must go to them for the standards of clarity they demanded. I also wish to thank Leo Rockas, my colleague at the University of Hartford, for his encouragement and helpful criticism. I am grateful to Margaret Hudnall for her kindness in volunteering to proofread the manuscript.

My father, D. Maurice Allan, was a great help on the philosophical background. I wish I had had the time and ability to profit by all of his suggestions for improving this aspect of my work. My wife Sally, as typist and editor, suggested many improvements in wording and provided sympathetic criticism.

6. "Rhyme and Reason: The Poetry of John Donne," *The Listener* 3 (March 19, 1930): 502.

Acknowledgments

I thank the publishers of the following for permission to quote from their publications:

The passage from John Dewey, "Reality and the Criterion for the Truth of Ideas," *Mind,* July 1907, is reprinted by permission of Basil Blackwell Publisher.

The passages from F. H. Bradley, *Appearance and Reality,* Second Edition; from F. H. Bradley, *Essays on Truth and Reality;* and from *The Works of Aristotle,* ed. W. D. Ross, are reprinted by permission of The Clarendon Press, Oxford.

The passages from the following titles by T. S. Eliot are reprinted by permission of Faber and Faber Ltd.: *Christianity and Culture; The Complete Poems and Plays, 1909–1950; Knowledge and Experience in the Philosophy of F. H. Bradley; On Poetry and Poets; Selected Essays,* Revised Edition; *To Criticize the Critic; The Use of Poetry and the Use of Criticism,* Second Edition; and unrepublished essays from *The Criterion.*

The passages from the following titles by T. S. Eliot are reprinted with the permission of Farrar, Straus and Giroux, Inc.: *On Poetry and Poets,* copyright © 1943, 1945, 1951, 1954, 1956, 1957 by T. S. Eliot; *To Criticize the Critic,* copyright © 1965 by Valerie Eliot; *Knowledge and Experience in the Philosophy of F. H. Bradley,* copyright © 1964 by T. S. Eliot.

13

Introduction

"A promising adolescent may revolt against the beliefs, the habits and the manners of his parents; but, in retrospect, we can see that he is also the continuer of their traditions, that he preserves essential family characteristics."[1] In Eliot's early criticism (which he himself later described as "the product of immaturity"), it is the signs of revolt against the nineteenth-century tradition that first command the attention.[2] But careful analysis of his early critical thought reveals that it shares a common basis with Romantic criticism and aesthetics; the central ideas of Eliot's criticism, also, originate in idealist epistemology. (The position set forth in Eliot's thesis on F. H. Bradley is in many respects strikingly similar to that which Coleridge expounded in the metaphysical chapters of *Biographia Literaria*.)

Eliot's conception of the role of personality in the composition and in the criticism of poetry perhaps best reveals on the one hand the continuity of his critical thought with that of the Romantics, and on the other his apparent determination either to fare forward or to retreat from the position Romantic criticism had reached in the work of Pater and his followers. The Romantics had found in idealist

1. T. S. Eliot, "What Is a Classic?" *On Poetry and Poets* (New York: Farrar, Straus and Giroux, 1961), p. 58.
2. "Preface to Edition of 1964," *The Use of Poetry and the Use of Criticism,* 2nd ed. (London: Faber and Faber, 1964), p. 10.

philosophy a way of restoring the human—indeed, the personal—to its place at the center of creation. It may need to be emphasized that Eliot began, logically as well as chronologically, at the same point at which the Romantics had begun. In 1927 he wrote, "What every poet starts from is his own emotions."[3] And eight years earlier, describing the proper stance of the critic, he had remarked, "To understand anything is to understand from a point of view."[4] It was not the idealist premise but certain conclusions drawn from it that Eliot rejected.

There was a definite tendency toward subjectivism in nineteenth-century idealism. This tendency brought with it certain problems—perhaps most of them could be listed under the topic "self-consciousness"—which appear to have disturbed Eliot profoundly. His resistance to this subjectivism was sometimes so strong as to obscure at least and perhaps to alter his fundamental adherence to idealism. Thus in his early criticism Eliot handled more roughly than any other opponent a critic—Walter Pater—many of whose critical concepts are quite like his own. So marked is Eliot's reaction against subjective idealism that J. Hillis Miller has written, "His career as a whole may be seen as an heroic effort to free himself from the limitation of nineteenth-century idealism and romanticism."[5]

As plausible and as helpful as Miller's argument is, I cannot share his confidence that Eliot's ultimate metaphysical position can be determined, and I should say that it is at least possible that what he takes to be revolt against idealism in general is revolt against subjective idealism. But it is not my purpose in this essay to try to answer such questions or to suggest that Eliot is really a Romantic in his

3. "Shakespeare and the Stoicism of Seneca," *Selected Essays*, 2nd ed. (New York: Harcourt, Brace and World, 1960), p. 117.
4. "Imperfect Critics," *The Sacred Wood*, 2nd ed. (London: Methuen, 1960), p. 38.
5. *Poets of Reality* (Cambridge: Harvard University Press, 1965), p. 179.

criticism; whatever the influence of nineteenth-century thought on Eliot, the importance for him of the criticism of the seventeenth and eighteenth centuries is at least as great. My purpose is to identify and explicate Eliot's basic critical concepts, and in these introductory pages I have been directing attention to the fact that these concepts originate in his study of idealist philosophy and that his application of these concepts is colored by his attitude toward idealism, a peculiar combination of attraction and revulsion.

T. S. Eliot's
Impersonal Theory
of Poetry

1
The Critical and Philosophical Background

This chapter is about certain critics and philosophers who influenced Eliot positively or against whom he reacted. There can be no question of an exhaustive treatment; one must hope that a discussion of a handful of writers can suggest in outline the immediate background against which Eliot's criticism should be seen.

One of the great problems of criticism has always been to define the degree to which literature should reflect the external world and the degree to which it should express or symbolize the personality of the writer. It is no accident, then, that starting at least as far back as Coleridge English criticism has been closely involved with idealist epistemology, which raises with regard to all knowledge just those same questions. In the idealist theory of knowledge, however, the concept of an "external" world does not remain an unexamined, or even a permissible, assumption. In critics influenced by idealism, therefore, the conflicting claims that criticism attempts to reconcile tend to be seen as those of poet and of society rather than as those of poet and of external world; since Coleridge, English criticism has tended to get drawn into sociology, as in the work of Matthew Arnold, Irving Babbitt, and Eliot himself. These

21

22   T. S. Eliot's Impersonal Theory of Poetry

writers involve criticism with one of the great topics of
English thought, "the old *aporia* of Authority *v.* Individual
Judgment," as Eliot called it.[1]

a. The Idealist Theory of Knowledge

It is necessary to start with a clear and comprehensive
statement of the idealist theory of knowledge. Plato's is apt
for our purposes.

> MENO: But how will you look for something when you don't
> in the least know what it is? How on earth are you going to set
> up something you don't know as the object of your search? To
> put it another way, even if you come right up against it, how
> will you know that what you have found is the thing you didn't
> know?
> SOCRATES: I know what you mean. Do you realize that what
> you are bringing up is the trick argument that a man cannot try
> to discover either what he knows or what he does not know?
> He would not seek what he knows, for since he knows it there
> is no need of the inquiry, nor what he does not know, for in
> that case he does not even know what he is too look for.
> MENO: Well, do you think it a good argument?
> SOCRATES: No.
> MENO: Can you explain how it fails?
> SOCRATES: I can. I have heard from men and women who
> understand the truths of religion. . . . The soul, since it is
> immortal and has been born many times, and has seen all
> things both here and in the other world, has learned everything
> that is. So we need not be surprised if it can recall the knowl-
> edge of virtue or anything else which, as we see, it once pos-
> sessed. All nature is akin, and the soul has learned everything,
> so that when a man has recalled a single piece of knowledge
> —*learned* it, in ordinary language—there is no reason why he
> should not find out all the rest, if he keeps a stout heart and
> does not grow weary of the search, for seeking and learning are
> in fact nothing but recollection.[2]

1. "The Frontiers of Criticism," *On Poetry and Poets* (New York:Farrar, Straus
and Giroux, 1961), p. 113.
2. *Meno,* 80d–81d, in *The Collected Dialogues of Plato,* ed. Edith Hamilton and

We may leave in the background the myth of recollection of a prenatal state and its relation to Romantic melancholy, "that inexhaustible discontent, languor, and homesickness . . . the chords of which ring all through our modern literature," which Pater found preeminently in Coleridge and which Eliot in his turn found that "Pater represents more positively than Coleridge."[3] The paradox that led to this myth may appear at first sight to be no more than a "trick argument," as Socrates called it. But his answer, it will be noticed, does not really impugn the validity of the paradox. Apparently it is possible for a modern philosopher to take it seriously. F. H. Bradley was, in effect, applying Plato's paradox when, in a passage quoted by Eliot, he ridiculed an empiricist's attempt to explain, through the theory of the association of ideas, how "an infant comes to recognize a lump of sugar."[4]

In his thesis on Bradley, Eliot asserted that "every perception involves some degree of recognition."[5] Years later, Eliot wrote, "We learn what poetry is—if we ever learn—from reading it; but one might say that we should not be able to recognise poetry in particular unless we had an innate idea of poetry in general."[6] When Bradley asserted "the ultimate identity of intenseness and extent" (i.e., intension and extension), he was restating the paradox of the *Meno* in the terms of modern logic.[7]

Bradley did not believe that the soul came to know the

Huntington Cairns (New York: Bollingen Foundation, 1963), pp. 363–64. Aristotle is not considered an idealist, but his doctrine that "actuality is prior to potentiality" (in the matter of knowledge, as elsewhere) is worth remembering, because it is perhaps closer to Eliot's position than is Plato's. See Sir David Ross, *Aristotle*, 5th ed. (London: Methuen, 1964), p. 177.

3. "Arnold and Pater," *Selected Essays*, 2nd ed. (New York: Harcourt, Brace and World, 1960), p. 393.

4. "Francis Herbert Bradley," *Selected Essays*, p. 396.

5. *Knowledge and Experience in the Philosophy of F. H. Bradley* (New York: Farrar, Straus and Company, 1964), p. 46. Cited hereafter as *Knowledge and Experience*.

6. *The Use of Poetry and the Use of Criticism*, 2nd ed. (London: Faber and Faber, 1964), p. 19. Cited hereafter as *The Use of Poetry*.

7. *Appearance and Reality*, 2nd ed. (Oxford: Clarendon Press, 1930), p. 390.

Ideas of all things in a prenatal state. But he believed that
the act of knowledge *precedes* our conscious awareness of
our knowledge, that it is the beginning as well as the end
of our "exploration." The last paragraph of the *Four Quart-
ests* is, in part, the poetic equivalent of Bradley's concept of
knowledge. According to Bradley the act of knowledge occurs in "immediate experience," a condition prior to, and
more real than, our conscious experience in terms of subject and object. Since by definition we can never be directly
aware of immediate experience, we may well ask how Bradley arrived at so unusual a doctrine. The answer is that he
saw it as the only possible alternative to the representational theory of knowledge, according to which we cannot
know things in themselves but only our ideas of them. This
theory was proposed by Descartes and thereafter had been
a basic assumption of many forms of idealism as well as of
the English empiricist school.[8] According to Bradley, this
theory leads to total scepticism: "If what we had at first
were the mere correlation [i.e., as against the identity] of
subject and object, then to rise beyond that would be impossible. From such premises there is in my opinion no
road except to total scepticism. This is the ground . . . on
which I may say that I have based myself always."[9]

The idealist theory of knowledge can easily be dissociated from the depreciation of the sensible world characteristic of Plato. For example, here is a passage in which
Pater explains what Raphael learned from Bartolommeo
and Da Vinci:

> Those masters of the ideal were for [Raphael], in the first
> instance, masters also of realism, as we say. Henceforth, to the
> end, he will be the analyst, the faithful reporter, in his work,
> of what he *sees*. He will realise the function of style as exem-
> plified in the practice of Da Vinci, face to face with the world

8. *Dictionary of Philosophy*, ed. Dagobert D. Runes (Ames, Iowa: Littlefield,
Adams and Company, 1955), p. 271.
9. *Essays on Truth and Reality* (Oxford: Clarendon Press, 1914), p. 199.

of nature and man as they are; selecting from, asserting one's self in a transcript of its veritable *data*; like drawing to like there, in obedience to the master's preference for the embodiment of the creative form within him.[10]

In fact, Kenneth Clark attributes to the influence of Pater the fact that Bradley rejected the tendency to rationalism in Hegel's philosophy, to which Bradley otherwise owed so much.[11] Bradley criticized Hegel in a famous passage also quoted by Eliot. "It may come from a failure in my metaphysics, or from a weakness of the flesh which continues to blind me, but the notion that existence could be the same as understanding strikes as cold and ghost-like as the dreariest materialism."[12] Bradley is here criticizing what Eliot would call the dissociation of sensibility, the separation of thought and sensation, both by Hegelian idealism and by materialism.

It will have been noticed that the Platonic view of knowledge, once purged of prejudice against sensation, is very suggestive of the concept of the "objective correlative." And in fact the author of a recent article has argued that the origin of the concept is to be found in Pater.[13] But if one has taken the trouble to trace the concept back to Pater, one might as well go on to Hegel and the last two of his three stages of art (Pater clearly indicated the source of his ideas):

> This unity, this perfect harmony between the idea and its external manifestation, constitutes the second form of art—the *Classic Form*.
> Here art has attained its perfection, in so far as there is

10. "Raphael," *The Renaissance*, intro. Kenneth Clark (Cleveland: World Publishing Company, 1961), p. 153.
11. "Introduction," *The Renaissance*, pp. 25–26.
12. "Francis Herbert Bradley," *Selected Essays*, p. 397.
13. David J. DeLaura, "Pater and Eliot: The Origin of the 'Objective Correlative,'" *Mod. Lang. Quart.*, 26 (1965): 426–31. DeLaura cites earlier studies that find the origin of the concept in Byron, Washington Allston, Nietzsche, and Husserl.

reached a perfect harmony between the idea as spiritual individuality, and the form as sensuous and corporal reality. . . .

Nevertheless, spirit cannot rest with this form, which is not its complete realization. . . . In the classic form, indeed, notwithstanding its generality, spirit . . . does not escape from the finite. . . .

It breaks up then this unity which forms the basis of Classic Art; it abandons the external world in order to take refuge within itself. This is what furnishes the type of the *Romantic Form*. Sensuous representation, with its images borrowed from the external world, no longer sufficing to express free spirituality, the form becomes foreign and indifferent to the idea.[14]

I do not cite Hegel as the ultimate source; instead I am suggesting that it is perhaps not worthwhile searching for any hypothetical ultimate source. In fact, I suppose that when Eliot wrote the famous sentences he did not think of himself as discovering an original formula. He probably expected some of his readers to realize that he was contradicting Hegel's (and Pater's) view that the Romantic is the art of the modern world.[15] There is a close connection between the theory of the objective correlative and the passage from Bradley cited in the note to line 412 of *The Waste Land*. It was taken from a chapter in which Bradley considers "the way of communication of souls." "It is certain, in the first place, that experiences [i.e., "finite centers of experience," which are, roughly, souls] are all separate from each other." From this it follows "that souls do not influence each other except through their bodies. And hence it is only by this way that they are able to communi-

14. "Selections from Lectures on Aesthetics," *The Philosophy of Hegel*, ed. Carl J. Friedrich (New York: Random House, 1953), pp. 334–35. Dryden's phrase "o'er-inform'd the tenement of clay" exactly expresses the production of Romantic Art, in Hegel's definition of it.

15. Frederick Copleston, *A History of Philosophy* (Part I) (Garden City, N.Y.: Doubleday and Company, 1965), 7: 279.

cate.''[16] So far we are very close to Eliot: "The only way of expressing emotion in the form of art is by finding an 'objective correlative' . . . such that when the external facts, which must terminate in sensory experience, are given, the emotion is immediately evoked.''[17] It is at this point that Bradley warns:

> But there is a natural mistake which, perhaps, I should briefly notice. Our inner worlds, I may be told, are divided from each other, but the outer world of experience is common to all; and it is by standing on this basis that we are able to communicate. Such a statement would be incorrect. My external sensations are no less private to myself than are my thoughts or my feelings. In either case my experience falls within my own circle, a circle closed on the outside; and, with all its elements alike, every sphere is opaque to the others which surround it. . . . In brief, regarded as an existence which appears in a soul, the whole world for each is peculiar and private to that soul. . . . Both our knowledge of sameness, and our way of communication, are indirect and inferential.[18]

This passage leads to consideration of the other side of Eliot's relation to idealist thought. However much influenced by it, he appears to have been profoundly disturbed by its tendency to subjectivism or solipsism. He was critical even of Bradley in this respect, though Bradley himself was opposed to subjectivism, as I shall explain below.[19] The anti-Romanticism of Eliot's early criticism is largely the expression of hostility to the kind of subjective idealism that we find in Pater.

16. *Appearance and Reality*, pp. 303–4.
17. "Hamlet and His Problems," *The Sacred Wood*, 2nd ed. (London: Methuen, 1960), p. 100, and *Selected Essays*, pp. 124–25.
18. *Appearance and Reality*, pp. 305–6. Cf. "Marina": "The pulse in the arm . . . more distant than stars and nearer than the eye."
19. "It is as difficult for Bradley as for Leibniz to maintain that there is any world at all, to find any objects for these mirrors [i.e., finite centres] to mirror." "Leibniz' Monads and Bradley's Finite Centres," in *Knowledge and Experience*, p. 202.

Let us examine a well-known passage from the "Conclu-sion" of *The Renaissance:* "The whole scope of observation is dwarfed into the narrow chamber of the individual mind. Experience, already reduced to a group of impressions, is ringed round for each one of us by that thick wall of person-ality through which no real voice has ever pierced on its way to us, or from us to that which we can only conjecture to be without. Every one of those impressions is the impres-sion of the individual in his isolation, each mind keeping as a solitary prisoner its own dream of a world."[20] Pater's subjective idealism almost literally justifies Eliot's hostile definition of Romanticism: "Romanticism is a short cut to the strangeness without the reality, and it leads its disciples only back upon themselves. George Wyndham had curi-osity, but he employed it romantically, not to penetrate the real world, but to complete the varied features of the world he made for himself."[21]

But Eliot's hostility to Pater cannot be explained simply as a result of his dislike of Pater's philosophical position. Remy de Gourmont also called himself a subjective idealist, and in the early criticism Eliot's praise of Gourmont is almost unqualified. Bradley's view is obviously similar to Pater's, though there is an important difference, which I shall discuss later. And Eliot wrote in his thesis that "my mind . . . is a point of view from which I cannot possibly escape (to which indeed I am bound so closely that the word escape is without meaning)."[22] Eliot's hostility to Pater is perhaps to be explained in practical terms. I think he attributed to Pater's influence the cult of personality that he attacked in the early criticism. In fact it seems possible that the the influence of Pater might cause in a disciple excessive self-consciousness. "Leonardo, brought up deli-

20. P. 221.
21. "Imperfect Critics," *The Sacred Wood,* pp. 31–32.
22. *Knowledge and Experience,* p. 145.

cately among the true children of that house, was the love-child of his youth, with the keen, puissant nature such children often have. We see him in his boyhood fascinating all men by his beauty, improvising music and songs, buying the caged birds and setting them free, as he walked the streets of Florence, fond of odd bright dresses and spirited horses."[23] One might think that no significant poet could owe much to Pater's influence—if there were not the example of Yeats. But Yeats's doctrine of the Mask seems to have come partly as a reaction against Pater. In *Dramatis Personae,* there are some notes of a speech to be given at the Arts Club: "Surely the ideal of culture expressed by Pater can only create feminine souls. The soul becomes a mirror not a brazier. . . . Culture of this kind produces the most perfect flowers in a few highbred women. It gives to its sons an exquisite delicacy. I will then compare the culture of the Renaissance, which seems to me founded not on self-knowledge but on knowledge of some other self, Christ or Caesar, not on delicate sincerity but on imitative energy."[24]

There are remarkable similarities between the criticism of Pater and that of Eliot, and the fact is readily explainable by their common heritage in the idealist tradition, in the school of Hegel. In view of this, I feel that Eliot was not quite fair to Pater—it may have been the very fact of the similarities that caused Eliot to insist on the distinction. For there is a basic distinction. Pater's "impressionism," his "repudiating any measure than man for all things," was certainly for Eliot a return of an old heresy in a new and dangerous form.[25] If Pater consciously revived the view-point of Heraclitus and Protagoras, Eliot consciously opposed that of Socrates to Pater and to his influence.

So far my analysis of idealism has been carried out only

---

23. "Leonardo da Vinci," *The Renaissance,* pp. 104–5.
24. *The Autobiography of William Butler Yeats* (New York: Macmillan Company, 1965), p. 323.
25. "Arnold and Pater," *Selected Essays,* p. 387.

to a point at which the positions of Bradley and Pater appear to be much the same, making something of a mystery Eliot's very different attitudes toward the two men. A brief sketch of the history of modern philosophy, however, will show that the position of Bradley is a distinct stage in the development of idealism beyond the subjective idealism of Pater.

I pointed out that the ground on which Bradley based himself was the necessity of finding an alternative to the scepticism inherent in the representational theory of knowledge: the theory that we cannot know things in themselves but only the "representations" of them in our minds. This theory was proposed by Descartes and became one of the basic assumptions of English empiricism. And, as Bertrand Russell puts it, "In Hume, the empiricist philosophy culminated in a scepticism which none could refute and none could accept."[26] Kant concluded that metaphysics is impossible; we can never know "things in themselves" because the mind imposes on sensations its own forms, the categories, such as time, space, and causality. I gather that much philosophy since Kant attempts to escape this dualism by taking either subject or object as primary and by explaining the other in terms of it. Thus in a thoroughgoing materialism, consciousness is reduced to an epiphenomenon. On the other hand, the great German idealists who came after Kant—Fichte, Schelling, and Hegel—attempted to redeem metaphysics by getting rid of "things in themselves" and reducing everything ultimately to subject: ego or reason or spirit.[27] They avoided solipsism, however, by going "behind the finite subject to a supraindividual intelligence, an absolute subject."[28] But in the next generation there was a tendency to reject a transcen-

---

26. *A History of Western Philosophy* (New York: Simon and Schuster, 1945), p. 494.
27. Copleston, *A History of Philosophy* 7 (Part 1): 15–49.
28. *Ibid.*, p. 18.

dent absolute and rest in subjective idealism. Walter Pater and Remy de Gourmont belong to this stage in the development of idealism. The most prominent names invoked by Gourmont in support of his subjective idealism are Schopenhauer and Nietzsche.[29]

Now we may consider, in its broadest outline, the position of Bradley. As Richard Wollheim puts it, "In traditional Idealist thought . . . the existence of Things, Time, Space, Cause, is denied only to make the world a freer place for the Self and God. In Bradley, however, the arguments that are used to dispossess material phenomena of reality are then turned against the phenomena of the spirit; the Self and God follow physical existences into the limbo of appearance."[30] Bradley's denial that the self is ultimately real is the step that advances beyond subjective idealism. The importance of this step can be shown by examining a sentence from a passage quoted above. "In brief, regarded as an existence which appears in a soul, the whole world for each is peculiar and private to that soul." This is a statement of subjective idealism, or even of solipsism, that is very close to the position of Pater. But for Bradley, to regard the world as an existence appearing *in* a soul is at best a half truth. For he also is determined to demonstrate that there is no essential self that can remain the same throughout life, unconditioned by the changing environment. Or, if there *is*, "this fixed essence not 'servile to all the skyey influences,' this wretched fraction and poor atom, too mean to be in danger—do you mean to tell me that this bare remnant is really the self? The supposition is preposterous."[31] In other words, in taking experience itself as prior to, and more real than, subject and object, Bradley occupied a position midway between *subjective idealism*, ac-

29. *Selected Writings*, trans. and ed. Glenn S. Burne (Ann Arbor: University of Michigan Press, 1966), p. 155.
30. *F. H. Bradley*, 2nd ed. (Baltimore: Penguin Books, 1969), p. 220.
31. *Appearance and Reality*, p. 69.

cording to which consciousness *is* the world, and *behaviorism,* according to which consciousness, in relationship to physiological process, is a mere epiphenomenon, i.e., "a by-product of a basic process which exerts no appreciable influence on the subsequent development of the process."[32] Eliot, in his thesis on Bradley, took just this position also. In chapter 5 below, I shall show that, in his early criticism, Eliot's denial of "the substantial unity of the soul" is directed against subjective idealism. In other words, the "Impersonal theory of poetry" is a criticism of just such a theory as Pater's.

Bradley rejected the first principles of German idealism. To him, the positing, as principles of explanation of the universe, of such absolute entities as Thought, Will, Ego, or Activity was a "gross superstition." Here he could be just as "positivistic" as the Empiricists. "Sentient experience, in short, is reality, and what is not this is not real."[33] For himself, he was sure that he had never experienced "Activity" or "Thought." "For in actual thinking we depend upon particular connexions, and, apart from this given matter, we should be surely unable to think."[34] It was here that he used the "polemical irony" Eliot described: "his habit of discomfiting an opponent with a sudden profession of ignorance, or inability to understand, or of incapacity for abstruse thought."[35]

The chapter that Bradley devoted, in *Appearance and Reality,* to a destructive analysis of the term *Activity* as a metaphysical principle is doubtless the model for Eliot's criticism of the word in "The Perfect Critic." We might briefly describe the attitude of both Bradley and Eliot by comparing it with that of Socrates in the *Symposium.* After the eulogies of Love as a pure force or a great god are completed,

32. *Dictionary of Philosophy,* p. 93.
33. *Appearance and Reality,* p. 127.
34. *Ibid.,* p. 423.
35. "Francis Herbert Bradley," *Selected Essays,* pp. 394–95.

Socrates clears away these notions with the simple step of forcing Agathon to admit that "Love is always the love of something."[36] "No one," Eliot wrote, "who had not witnessed the event could imagine the conviction in the tone of Professor Eucken as he pounded the table and exclaimed *Was ist Geist? Geist ist . . .*"[37] Anyone who has read Eliot's thesis will suspect, I believe, that it was Eliot himself who asked that socratic question, *"Was ist Geist?"*

It is perhaps even possible to see Bradley in the Empiricist tradition. He was able to declare his "agreement with the English school at its best."[38] As Eliot put it, "People are inclined to believe that what Bradley did was to demolish the logic of Mill and the psychology of Bain. . . . If he had done that it would have been less of a service than people think, for there is much that is good in the logic of Mill and the psychology of Bain. . . . His force is directed not against Mill's logic as a whole but only against certain limitations, imperfections and abuses."[39]

Bradley's position is called "idealism" in part because it opposes materialism: Reality is experience. But that is not enough to place him beyond doubt in the idealist tradition; his position, as I have explained it so far, is remarkably like that of David Hume. In order to see what sustains Bradley's idealism, we can best begin by realizing what he yielded of traditional idealism. At first sight it seems that he gave away almost everything. There is no longer any transcendent world of Reality behind and separate from our ordinary reality. "The real is that which is known in presentation or intuitive knowledge. It is that which we encounter in feeling or perception. Again it is that which appears in the series

---

36. *The Collected Dialogues of Plato,* p. 553 (200e). Of course, both Plato and Bradley go beyond this "positivism" to construct positions in some ways as remote from direct experience as the "superstitions" they attacked.

37. "The Perfect Critic," *The Sacred Wood,* p. 9.

38. *Collected Essays* (Oxford: Clarendon Press, 1935), 1: 206.

39. "Francis Herbert Bradley," *Selected Essays,* pp. 397–98.

of events that occur in space and time."[40] There is no
"Universal Mind." "Certainly for me beyond and outside
of all finite minds there is no truth. From the doctrine
which I inherited all such transcendence has in principle
been banished."[41] From the broadest view, it appears that
there is, in Bradley, only one doctrine that sustains idealism: his insistence that there is a *formal criterion of truth.* I
shall examine this criterion shortly. But first a passage by
John Dewey should be helpful in placing the significance,
as it appeared to his contemporaries, of Bradley's idealism,
both in what it yielded and in what it retained.

> Among the influences that have worked in contemporary phi-
> losophy towards disintegration of intellectualism of the epis-
> temological type, and towards the substitution of a philosophy
> of experience, the work of Mr. Bradley must be seriously
> counted. One has, for example, only to compare his metaphy-
> sics with the two fundamental contentions of T. H. Green
> [Bradley's "master"], namely, that reality is a single, eternal
> and all-inclusive system of relations, and that this system of
> relations is essentially one with that process of relating which
> constitutes our thinking, to be instantly aware of a changed
> atmosphere, and to call to mind how much of Bradley's writ-
> ings is a sustained and deliberate polemic against intellectual-
> ism of the Neo-Kantian type. When, however, we find con-
> joined with this criticism an equally sustained contention that
> the philosophic conception of reality must be wholly based on
> an exclusively intellectual criterion, a criterion belonging to
> and confined to theory, we have a situation as perplexing as it
> is thought-provoking.[42]

Here is Bradley's formal criterion of truth: "If you think
at all so as to discriminate between truth and falsehood,
you will find that you cannot accept open self-contradic-

40. *The Principles of Logic,* 2nd ed. (London: Oxford University Press, 1922), 1:
44.
41. *Essays on Truth and Reality,* p. 349.
42. "Reality and the Criterion for the Truth of Ideas," *Mind* n.s.16 (July 1907):
317.

tion. Hence to think is to judge, and to judge is to criticize, and to criticize is to use a criterion of reality." As the last sentence indicates, this principle of noncontradiction or self-consistency is not only a criterion of truth; Bradley made the important step of assuming that it is also a criterion of Reality. "Ultimate reality is such that it does not contradict itself; here is an absolute criterion."[43] This criterion is *a priori* in the sense that it cannot be denied by our experience; in fact, Bradley's Absolutism rests on the assumption that our ordinary experience *is* self-contradictory or inconsistent. If we did not become aware that reality as it *appears* to us is inconsistent, we could never go beyond it, for we never experience anything except appearances.

Let me try to approach the significance of the formal criterion of truth from another angle. Bradley's effort was to revive metaphysics in England, to demonstrate that we can say *something* meaningful about the universe as a whole and are not confined, as the empiricists would have it, to describing what goes on in the "human understanding." For Bradley, the revival of metaphysics had to rest on the recognition that logic, the science of the *form* of knowledge, is valid in itself and is not a mere derivative of psychology or associationism. As we have seen, other roads of escape from the psychological attitude were closed to Bradley. There is in his view no transcendent world of reason or spirit separate from our ordinary reality, as in earlier versions of idealism, and there is no "external" world of objects independent of subjects, as in realism. For Bradley, Reality is appearance—the ordinary reality we experience —but appearance transformed, its contradictions harmonized into one consistent system.

The significance of logic is well expressed by A. E. Taylor, a disciple of Bradley, in his reply to an attack on it from the school of pragmatism (heirs of empiricism): "[Mr.

43. *Appearance and Reality*, p. 120.

Sturt] more than once denounces vigorously the very proposal to separate the study of Logic from Psychology and . . . he entertains for Formal Logic a contempt which he makes no attempt to hide. Now a writer who declares that Logic ought to be founded on Psychology is in fact saying that what we ought to believe is true can be ascertained simply by an inquiry into what we do actually believe, and from this position the advance to the conclusion that a proposition may acquire the right to be believed by the mere fact of being actually believed, by a sort of 'prescription,' seems an inevitable and obvious step."[44]

Bradley believed, then, that by imposing order on our experience, by correcting it in accordance with the criterion of self-consistency, we escape the bounds of subjectivity and advance part way, at least, toward Reality. But even if we could make our experience completely self-consistent we should still not be satisfied. For there is a second criterion: we do not accept as true what does not satisfy us as the "objective correlative" of the purely felt quality of our experience. We are presented with a dilemma. We achieve a world of interrelations and thus of meaning only through reflection; such a world is therefore ideal and not real. But let no one say that what is prior to reflection is the "external" world of fact. What is prior to reflection is the immediate experience of the present moment, and Bradley agrees that this deserves the adjective *real* in a way that nothing else does. However, without the work of reflection, immediate experience would yield only a series of isolated moments "with no before and after." No one but an empiricist philosopher would accept such a world as real. For Bradley, only that which has at once the immediacy and unity of pure feeling and the comprehensiveness and self-consistency of pure thought is worthy of the name Reality.

44. [A review of] *Idola Theatri, a Criticism of Oxford Thought and Thinkers*, by Henry Sturt, *Mind* n.s. 16 (July 1907): 425.

But we can never get feeling and thought to come together except briefly and occasionally (as in art). Nevertheless, we must try to reconcile feeling and thought without sacrificing one to the other. In short, we find in Bradley a model for that peculiar combination of intellectualism and anti-intellectualism which we think of as characteristic of Eliot. Eliot's statement of the function of art corresponds exactly to Bradley's conception of the function of metaphysics: "For it is ultimately the function of art, in imposing a credible order upon ordinary reality, and thereby eliciting some perception of an order *in* reality, to bring us to a condition of serenity, stillness, and reconciliation; and then leave us, as Virgil left Dante, to proceed toward a region where that guide can avail us no farther."[45]

Seen in its overall outlines, Eliot's position vis-à-vis romantic aesthetics is analogous to Bradley's position vis-à-vis the German idealism of the first half of the nineteenth century. Eliot believed that literature should deal with ordinary reality and not with an "artificial world" but that it must not degenerate into realism.[46] And literature is to be sustained at a level above realism not, as in Romantic theory, by Imagination but by Form.

To John Dewey, Bradley's version of idealism, sustained only by a formal criterion of truth, appeared to be a futile last stand of idealism.

The cynically-minded are moved to wonder whether this tremendous insistence upon one factor in present experience at the expense of others, is not because this is the only way to maintain the notion of 'Absolute Experience,' and to prevent it from collapsing into ordinary every-day experience. In any case the thesis I wish to maintain is that Mr. Bradley's Absolute Experience, resting ultimately upon a rationalistic conception of the criterion of truth, is a temporary half-way house into

45. "Poetry and Drama," *On Poetry and Poets,* p. 94.
46. *Ibid.,* p. 87.

which travellers from the territory of Kantian epistemology
may temporarily turn aside in their journey towards the land
of a philosophy of every-day experience.[47]

Before moving on to consider Remy de Gourmont, I
would point out that Eliot's early interest in Oriental philosophy appears to be related to his interest in Bradley. So
far as Oriental philosophy is concerned, I have done little
more than attempt to hold the eel of science by the tail. The
table of contents, particularly for chapter 2, of Henry
Clarke Warren's *Buddhism in Translations* (which Eliot
recommended in the notes to *The Waste Land*) suggests
many similarities to Bradley's doctrines. For example,
there are headings such as "There is no Ego" and "No
continuous Personal Identity."[48]

If one comes to Remy de Gourmont in the original only
after first making his acquaintance through Eliot, one is
likely to be somewhat disappointed—or relieved, as the
case may be. One had expected a mind austere, impersonal,
and highly serious. Instead, Gourmont is garrulous, expan-
sive, modish, impressionistic, personal, a frank sensualist.
To the influence of Remy de Gourmont, more than to any
other, can be traced the great emphasis on sensation in
Eliot's early criticism. Here is a typical passage from *Le
Problème du style:*

> *Nihil intellectu quod non prius fuerit in sensu:* the senses are
> the unique doorway through which enters all that lives in the
> mind, the very notion of consciousness, and the very feeling of
> personality. An idea is only a faded sensation, an effaced im-
> age. . . . If feeling does not intervene in the manipulation of
> ideas, it is pure parroting. . . . Reasoning by means of sensorial
> images is much easier and much more certain than reasoning
> by ideas. . . . Philosophy, which passes in average minds for the

47. "Reality and the Criterion for the Truth of Ideas," *Mind,* n.s. 16 (July 1907):
318.
48. *Buddhism in Translations* (New York: Atheneum, 1963), p. ix.

domain of pure ideas (those chimeras!), is lucid only when conceived and written by sensorial writers. . . .

Sensation is the basis of everything, of the moral and intellectual life as well as the physical life. Two hundred and fifty years after Hobbes, two hundred years after Locke, such has been the destructive power of religious Kantism that one is reduced to insisting on such elementary aphorisms.[49]

Nevertheless, Gourmont was an apostle of a doctrine he called indifferently "phenomenalism" or "subjective idealism."[50] We saw in the case of Pater that idealism is not incompatible with sensationalism, and in fact Gourmont's philosophical position is very close to that of Pater. Gourmont claimed that phenomenalism was the philosophical basis of the Symbolist movement. In an essay in which he proposed to define Symbolism, Gourmont wrote:

A new truth . . . has recently appeared in literature and art. . . . This truth—evangelical and marvelous, liberating and rejuvenating—is the principle of the ideality of the world. In relation to man (the thinking subject), the world (all that is exterior to the self) exists only as the idea formed of it. We know only phenemena; we can reason only about appearances. All truth, in itself, escapes us. The essence is unattainable. This is what Schopenhauer has popularized in that clear and simple formula: the world is my representation. . . . It is the universal principle of emancipation for all men capable of comprehending.[51]

There is some confirmation for this interesting interpretation of Symbolism in Arthur Symons's *The Symbolist Movement in Literature:* "Fundamentally, the belief of Villiers is

49. *Selected Writings*, pp. 122–23.
50. "[The idealism] which Nietzsche has carried to the point of phenomenalism, is a philosophical conception of the world. Schopenhauer, who did not invent it, has given it the best formulation: the world is my representation—that is, the world is such as it appears to me. If it has a real existence in itself, it is inaccessible to me. It is what I see it, or feel it, to be." *Selected Writings*, p. 155.
51. *Ibid.*, p. 181.

the belief common to all Eastern mystics. 'Know, once for all, that there is for thee no other universe than that conception thereof which is reflected at the botton of thy thoughts.' " And Symons quotes Verlaine: "I am far from sure that the philosophy of Villiers will not one day become the formula of our century."[52] It is probable that the countless references to Platonic recollection in late nineteenth-century literature and criticism are to be interpreted as metaphors for subjective idealism. Observe that, in the passage from the *Meno* quoted at the beginning of this chapter, the myth of recollection follows logically from, and is offered as the solution to, the problem of knowledge and is perhaps not intended as a scientific solution.

The charge that this doctrine of subjective idealism leaves no external criterion of truth Gourmont accepts willingly: "The work of a writer must be not only the reflection, but the enlarged reflection, of his personality. The only excuse a man has for writing is to write himself—to reveal to others the kind of world reflected in his individual mirror. . . . We acknowledge, then, that Symbolism . . . is the expression of individualism in art."[53]

At this point in the discussion we are faced with two questions. Why did Eliot apparently overlook in Gourmont the subjectivism he would have censured in Pater? ("We should be thankful that Walter Pater did not fix his attention on this play" [Hamlet].[54]) Second, how do we reconcile the individualism, the emphasis on personality, of Gourmont with Eliot's "Impersonal theory of poetry"? I think that the answer to these questions is the same. For Gourmont personality is ultimately physiological. "The real problem of style is a question of physiology. . . . We

52. *The Symbolist Movement in Literature,* rev. ed. (New York: E. P. Dutton and Company, 1958), p. 23.

53. *Selected Writings,* pp. 181–82.

54. "Hamlet and His Problems," *The Sacred Wood,* p. 95, and *Selected Essays,* p. 121.

write, as we feel, as we think, with our entire body."[55] The great emphasis on physiology in Gourmont would serve to compensate for his subjectivism. In his thesis on Bradley, Eliot several times presents his own position as midway between subjective idealism and behaviorism.[56]

The rapprochement of idealism and materialism in Gourmont is typical of the spirit of the times and worth illustrating further. In 1904 he wrote an essay, "The Roots of Idealism," in which he asked himself whether he ought not to reverse his view, whether Lamarck was not right in saying that "the environment creates the organ [i.e., of sensation]."[57] He concluded that the question was indifferent, that both idealism and materialism come to the same thing insofar as they are opposed to rationalism: "Idealism is definitely founded on the very materiality of thought, considered as a physiological product. The conception of an external world that is exactly knowable is compatible only with the belief in reason, that is, in the soul, that is, moreover, in the existence of an immutable, incorruptible, immortal principle, whose judgments are infallible."[58] This is to be compared with Eliot: "The point of view which I am struggling to attack is perhaps related to the metaphysical theory of the substantial unity of the soul."[59] The quota-

55. *Selected Writings*, p. 109.

56. "The point of view from which each soul is a world in itself must not be confused with the point of view from which each soul is only a function of a physical organism. . . . And yet these two souls are the same. And if the two points of view are irreconcilable, yet on the other hand neither would exist without the other, and they melt into each other by a process which we cannot grasp." "Liebniz' Monads and Bradley's Finite Centres," in *Knowledge and Experience*, pp. 205–6. Eliot retained throughout his career the *form* of this analysis: orthodoxy is always seen as a mean that cannot be conceptualized between two intelligible but unacceptable extremes. See *Selected Essays*, p. 230.

57. *Selected Writings*, p. 155.

58. *Ibid.*, p. 167. Similarly Eliot referred to "the materialism, which (as exemplified particularly in the work of Mr. Bosanquet) from one point of view may very justly be said to lie at the basis of idealism." *Knowledge and Experience*, p. 153.

59. "Tradition and the Individual Talent," *The Sacred Wood*, p. 56, and *Selected Essays*, p. 9.

tions will show further how the individualism of Gourmont may lie behind the "Impersonal theory of poetry."

It is my impression that Remy de Gourmont is the fundamental critical source of Imagism. Glenn S. Burne remarks that "much in Hulme's *Speculations* appears to be paraphrased from *Le Problème du style.*"[60] A survey of Hulme's work suggests that Burne is right. It is of course unnecessary to demonstrate the debt of Pound, Aldington, and Amy Lowell to Gourmont. Therefore, I shall not discuss these writers at length.

However, it is worth noticing that Amy Lowell's version of Imagism appears to have involved a reaction against idealism. In 1916 she remarked of the several groups of new poets that they "have certain traits which they hold in common, and which separate them from the poets immediately preceding them. Chief among these is 'externality,' the regarding of the world as having existence apart from one-self. Introspection is not the besetting sin of the new poets, as it was of the poets of the nineties."[61] But I have not been able to find in Pound or Hulme definite evidence that Imagism for them implied a realistic epistemology.

When, in 1927, Eliot wrote his essay on Bradley, he recognized that the neorealism of Bertrand Russell and G. E. Moore had succeeded in undermining the position of idealism as the dominant philosophy in the English universities. Russell has described the exhilaration he felt when "towards the end of 1898 . . . Moore and I rebelled against both Kant and Hegel." "I felt it, in fact, as a great liberation, as if I had escaped from a hot-house on to a windswept headland. I hated the stuffiness involved in supposing that space and time were only in my mind."[62]

We have seen above that one of the most powerful motives in Eliot's early criticism is reaction against one ver-

60. "Introduction," *Selected Writings*, p. 5.

61. Samuel Foster Damon, *Amy Lowell* (New York and Boston: Houghton Mifflin Company, 1935), p. 351.

62. *My Philosophical Development* (New York: Simon and Schuster, 1959), pp. 54, 61–62.

sion, at least, of idealism. We even find Eliot, shortly after completing his thesis, dissociating himself to some degree from Bradley himself: "He has expounded one type of philosophy with such consummate ability that it will probably not survive him."[63] Any interpretation of Eliot's criticism must at some point face the question of whether or not Eliot eventually abandoned idealism.

In *Poets of Reality,* J. Hillis Miller has, in fact, interpreted Eliot's career as "an heroic effort to free himself from the limitations of nineteenth-century idealism and romanticism," the turning point toward success being Eliot's acceptance of Christianity.[64] Miller's interpretation is the most acute attempt to relate Eliot's thesis to his criticism and poetry that I have found. Although I am not ready to assent to all of the steps in Miller's argument, I agree that a turn toward some form of realism, with the help of Christian theology, is a possibility that must be considered in any interpretation of Eliot. My own opinion is that we may never be able to determine Eliot's final metaphysical position (if there is one), for the reason that, before reaching the point at which (in Miller's view) Eliot should have succeeded in rejecting idealism, an even more fundamental change had occurred in his critical approach: he had purified his critical vocabulary of metaphysical assumptions, if not entirely, at least well enough so that it does not imply any one philosophical position. By 1964 Eliot professed to be no longer able to understand the terminology of his thesis.[65]

I turn now to a problem—that of the source of authority —implicit in any form of idealism and particularly acute in subjective idealism such as that of Pater and Gourmont. I shall examine the attempts to solve this problem by two men, Arnold and Babbitt, who start with an individualism much like that of Pater and Gourmont but who have power-

63. "Leibniz' Monads and Bradley's Finite Centres," in *Knowledge and Experience,* p. 207.
64. *Poets of Reality* (Cambridge: Harvard University Press, 1965), p. 179.
65. *Knowledge and Experience,* p. 10.

ful motives for reaching out to some external, objective source of authority. Since neither man had confidence in the continuing efficiency of Religion as the source of authority, both looked to Culture to supply its place. The heavy burden of responsibility such a program tended to place on literature raised vexing problems for criticism.

b. The Search for Authority

Of that part of Matthew Arnold's work with which Eliot was sympathetic, the essence is perhaps in sections of "The Function of Criticism at the Present Time" and in "The Literary Influence of Academies," and the quintessence in the following sentences:

> Therefore, a nation whose chief spiritual characteristic is energy, will not be very apt to set up, in intellectual matters, a fixed standard, an authority, like an academy. By this it certainly escapes certain real inconveniences and dangers, and it can, at the same time, as we have seen, reach undeniably splendid heights in poetry and science. On the other hand, some of the requisites of intellectual work are specially the affair of quickness of mind and flexibility of intelligence. The form, the method of evolution, the precision, the proportions, the relations of the parts to the whole, in an intellectual work, depend mainly upon them. And these are the elements of an intellectual work which are really most communicable from it, which can most be learned and adopted from it, which have, therefore, the greatest effect upon the intellectual performance of others. Even in poetry, these requisites are very important; and the poetry of a nation, not eminent for the gifts on which they depend, will, more or less, suffer by this shortcoming. In poetry, however, they are, after all, secondary, and energy is the first thing; but in prose they are of first-rate importance. . . . These are what, as I have said, can to a certain degree be learned and appropriated, while the free activity of genius cannot.[66]

66. "The Literary Influence of Academies," *Essays in Criticism,* 2nd ed. (New York: Dutton, 1964), pp. 40–41.

Eliot's tribute to Arnold is virtually a paraphrase of this:

> After the prophetic frensies of the end of the eighteenth and the beginning of the nineteenth century, he seems to come to us saying: 'This poetry is very fine, it is opulent and careless, it is sometimes profound, it is highly original; but you will never establish and maintain a tradition if you go on in this haphazard way. There are minor virtues which have flourished better at other times and in other countries: these you must give heed to, these you must apply, in your poetry, in your prose, in your conversation and your way of living; else you condemn yourselves to enjoy only fitful and transient bursts of literary brilliance, and you will never, as a people, a nation, a race, have a fully formed tradition and personality.'[67]

It is precisely here that Eliot's admiration for English literature of the seventeenth and eighteenth centuries fits in: "It is not, as is often said, that English literature is merely a collection of isolated and freakish men of genius; there was a long tradition from Ben Jonson through Dryden, down to Samuel Johnson and perhaps a little later; there was another tradition from Locke."[68] Yet, for Arnold, "Dryden and Pope are not classics of our poetry, they are classics of our prose."[69] The last two sentences of the paragraph from Arnold quoted above show the critical ambivalence that fifteen years later was to result in this formula.

Arnold's view of Dryden and Pope as the "classics of our prose" has at least this virtue: it points to the fact that though the spirit of the eighteenth century is not much present in the poetry of the nineteenth, it is often to be felt in the *prose* of that century—and of the twentieth also—not least in the prose of Matthew Arnold. Eliot once noted of A. E. Housman that "he is both a nineteenth (or twentieth) century romantic poet and an eighteenth-century wit."[70]

67. *The Use of Poetry*, pp. 104–5.
68. "A Preface to Modern Literature," *Vanity Fair*, 21 (November 1923): 118.
69. "The Study of Poetry," *Essays in Criticism*, p. 253.
70. "[A review of] *The Name and Nature of Poetry*," *The Criterion*, 13 (October 1933): 152.

Arnold's valuation of Dryden and Pope is, as Eliot said of his valuation of the Romantic poets, "very much influenced by his religious attitude."[71] "We should conceive of poetry worthily," Arnold declared, "and more highly than it has been the custom to conceive of it. We should conceive of it as capable of higher uses, and called to higher destinies, than those which in general men have assigned to it hitherto. . . . Most of what now passes with us for religion and philosophy will be replaced by poetry."[72] It is obvious that Dryden and Pope will not be able to survive in this kind of atmosphere. Conversely, Arnold's attitude explains why Eliot so often specified a taste for Dryden and Pope as a test for genuine enjoyment of poetry *as poetry*.

I need not discuss in detail Eliot's long critical campaign against the substitution of poetry for religion, waged against Arnold himself and against subsequent proponents, such as I. A. Richards. Leaving religion to take care of itself, we may consider the probable effects of this substitution on the study of literature. I find myself, somewhat reluctantly, in agreement with Eliot. It can almost be said that there is a logical fallacy in Arnold's critical program, that the idea of poetry as religion and the idea of criticism as "a *disinterested* endeavor to learn and propagate the best that is known and thought in the world" are necessarily incompatable.[73]

The antithesis of energy to intelligence in the long passage from Arnold with which I began this section indicates that the polarity of poetry and prose is related to that of Hebraism and Hellenism, though the two polarities are not perfectly congruent, of course. Finally in Arnold's passage we might note the implied identification of energy and poetry with individualism, and of prose and intelligence

---

71. *The Use of Poetry*, p. 110.
72. "The Study of Poetry," *Essays in Criticism*, p. 235.
73. "The Function of Criticism," *Essays in Criticism*, p. 32. (Italics mine.)

with acceptance of social authority. Keeping these complexes of ideas in mind, we may turn to *Culture and Anarchy* for further illumination of them.

Almost immediately we run into difficulties. How is it that a way of life based on the law of *obedience* (Hebraism) has fostered an attitude of "doing as one likes"? And how is it that Hellenism, encouraging "spontaneity of consciousness," works against this same liberty of "doing as one likes"? Of course one is aware that there are *facts* of English social and religious history that give Arnold's analysis a certain plausibility, but that does not obviate the necessity for logical consistency. The situation becomes somewhat clearer when we notice, what Arnold seems reluctant to say unequivocally, that Hellenism encourages scepticism. "And as the force which encourages us to stand staunch and fast by the rule and ground we have is Hebraism, so the force which encourages us to go back upon this rule, and to try the very ground on which we appear to stand, is Hellenism,—a turn for giving our consciousness free play and enlarging its range."[74] But the fact remains, I think it must be admitted, that Dryden, Swift, and Hume analyzed these problems more cogently and more succinctly than Arnold, and that *Culture and Anarchy* cannot be fully understood unless it is seen as part of a long tradition. I am tempted to say that the problem of authority is *the* great topic of English thought.

Culture and Anarchy may be regarded, then, as a restatement in contemporary terms of the search for authority as analyzed in *Religio Laici, A Tale of a Tub,* and Hume's essay "Of Superstition and Enthusiasm" (to name only a few of the relevant works). Perhaps the most cogent logical analysis of the problem is in Hume's brief essay (though, from a historical point of view, one notices his failure to foresee

74. *Culture and Anarchy,* ed. J. Dover Wilson (Cambridge: Cambridge University Press, 1960), pp. 150–51.

the revival and persistence of nonconformity). There are *three* conceptions of the source of authority. At one extreme is Enthusiasm, dogmatic individualism, contempt of social authority sustained by confidence that one is in direct communion with God. This is what Arnold called Hebraism. At the other extreme is Superstition, authoritarian dogmatism. And between these there is—what? In religion it is the self-professed Anglican way.[75] I certainly do not presume to offer a definitive formula for the Anglican way, but it is hard to avoid the impression that in 1688 the English people entered into a contract with God as well as with the King and that they expected the former also to consider himself limited by this contract. Certainly, the middle way implies, in comparison with the extremes, some degree of scepticism; this is clear in Dryden and even in Swift. It is also clear that the Anglican way tends to locate the source of authority in convention, in society. Finally, these two tendencies—scepticism and convention—go together; scepticism operating on Enthusiasm (Enthusiasm having already vanquished Superstition) leads to convention. Or, in Arnold's terms, Hellenism, turning a free play of ideas upon Hebraism, leads to the acceptance of the authority of Culture.

I think we must recognize that, by conscious intention and perhaps also because of unconscious ambivalence, there has been a tendency in spokesmen for the middle way to avoid a definitive formula for authority that should unequivocally reject either Enthusiasm or Superstition. In 1948 Eliot observed that "the Church of England itself has comprehended wider variations of belief and cult than a foreign observer would believe it possible for one institu-

75. "The Church of England is undoubtedly both as to doctrine and worship the purest church that is at this day in the world: the most orthodox in faith, the freest on the one hand from idolatry and superstition, and on the other hand from freakishness and enthusiasm, of any now extant." Archbishop Sharp of York, quoted by Peter Gay, *The Enlightenment* (New York: Alfred A. Knopf, 1966), p. 346.

tion to contain without bursting.''[76] It is certainly true, as we shall see, that Arnold falls into apparent inconsistencies in his attempts to define the source of authority. But I think it likely that Eliot's real objection to Arnold's efforts is not that Arnold is too ambivalent but that he is not ambivalent enough. At least, Eliot's earliest explicit attempt to define the source of authority, in the essay of 1923, "The Function of Criticism," is not without some of the ambivalence of Arnold and, in fact, like *Culture and Anarchy*, is not fully intelligible, I think, until it is put into its place within the central tradition of English thought, although it professes to criticize that tradition from without.

At the beginning of this essay, Eliot seems, by rejecting the position of J. M. Murry, to affirm what Hume would call Superstitition, "the principle of unquestioned spiritual authority outside the individual."[77] (The position he affirms in criticism he calls Classicism, and he recognizes it as analogous to Catholicism in religion.) But then he admits that there is much difficulty in defining the terms *outside* and *inside*. And at the end of the essay we find a formula for authority, at least in criticism, that would have satisfied Hume and Arnold: "For the kinds of critical work which we have admitted, there is the possibility of co-operative activity, with the further possibility of arriving at something outside of ourselves, which may provisionally be called truth."[78] This is, in fact, the best short formula for the middle way that I know of.

As a statement of Eliot's concept of the source of authority in criticism, this formula is definitive. Almost everyone will disagree with some or many of Eliot's critical judgments, but so far as anyone sees Eliot's criticism as dogmatic, that will be a function of his own superstition or

---

76. *Notes towards the Definition of Culture,* in *Christianity and Culture* (New York: Harcourt, Brace and Company, 1949), p. 147.
77. "The Function of Criticism," *Selected Essays,* p. 15.
78. *Ibid.,* p. 22.

enthusiasm, a function of the degree to which he partakes either in "the ineradicable tendency of the great majority of men to repeat the opinions of those few who have taken the trouble to think" or in "the tendency of a nimble but myopic minority to progenerate heterodoxies."[79] Now it is true that, for Eliot, the problems raised by these tendencies require for their solution the periodic advent of a literary "dictator." It is also true that, for reasons we shall examine in a later chapter, Eliot had a peculiarly strong motive for opposing critical pyrrhonism or impressionism. Nevertheless, the attentive reader will find in Eliot's criticism, as in the essays of David Hume, a continual implicit suggestion that he should first think for himself and that he should then engage in "co-operative activity."

If we turn from criticism to other areas of Eliot's thought —to religion and morals, for example—we can no longer affirm so confidently that Eliot takes the "middle way." (Religion and morals are relevant to Eliot's criticism proper in a way that he himself stated exactly: "Literary criticism should be completed by criticism from a definite ethical and theological standpoint. . . . The 'greatness' of literature cannot be determined solely by literary standards; though we must remember that whether it is literature or not can be determined only by literary standards."[80]) A detailed analysis of Eliot's search for a principle of authority will be made in chapter 5. Eliot may never have taken a definitive position. He seems to have had a significant tendency toward, and even a sympathy for, *all* of the conceptions of the source of authority we have considered, not excluding those he sometimes strongly censured. In 1955 Eliot recognized as operative elements of his own critical taste: "a Catholic cast of mind, a Calvinistic heritage, and a Puritanical temperament."[81]

79. *The Use of Poetry*, p. 109.
80. "Religion and Literature," *Selected Essays*, p. 343.
81. "Goethe as the Sage," *On Poetry and Poets*, p. 243.

It is likely that Eliot differs from Arnold, and even from Hume, not so much by having arrived at a definite intellectual position clearly distinguishable from theirs as by having a greater sympathy for "superstition" and, for that matter, for "enthusiasm." I emphasize the word *intellectual,* because it is obvious that Eliot's faith itself is of an entirely different order from Arnold's. Eliot said of him, "Perhaps he cared too much for civilisation, forgetting that Heaven and Earth shall pass away, and Mr. Arnold with them, and there is only one stay."[82] Eliot objects, not to Arnold's scepticism, but to his not being sceptical enough of the efficacy of Culture. "The total effect of Arnold's philosophy is to set up Culture in the place of Religion."[83] (This is precisely the same objection Eliot made to Babbitt's Humanism.) In partial support of Eliot's criticism, we may observe that Arnold's position is rather too obviously equivalent to that of Swift's amusing opponent of "the abolishing of Christianity": "Nor do I think it wholly groundless, or my fears altogether imaginary, that the abolishing of Christianity may perhaps bring the Church in danger, or at least put the senate to the trouble of another securing vote." Furthermore, Arnold appears to have been capable of suppressing any sense of the irony of such a position.

Eliot suggested that the incoherence of Arnold's position enabled it to father two very different offspring: Humanism and "the view of life of Walter Pater."[84] Before turning to the Humanism of Irving Babbitt, I shall comment briefly on Arnold's relation to Pater.

Eliot suggested that Arnold's position, though less outspokenly than Pater's, had the same effect of "repudiating any measure than man for all things."[85] There is evidence to support this interpretation, for example, Arnold's trib-

82. *The Use of Poetry,* p. 119.
83. "Arnold and Pater," *Selected Essays,* p. 387.
84. *Ibid.,* pp. 384–85
85. *Ibid.,* p. 387.

ute to Goethe in "Heinrich Heine": "Goethe's profound, imperturbable naturalism is absolutely fatal to all routine thinking; he puts the standard, once for all, inside every man instead of outside him."[86] Now, though Arnold himself usually avoids stating his position in metaphysical terms, we may yet say that he was at least aware that this sceptical humanism could be grounded in subjective idealism. Just before making this tribute to Goethe, Arnold had quoted Goethe himself: "Through me the German poets have become aware that, as a man must live from within outwards, so the artist must work from within outwards, seeing that, make what contortions he will, he can only bring to light his own individuality."[87]

Yet, in the "Conclusion" to *Culture and Anarchy*, Arnold could plume himself on being harder on radical dissent than even the Philistines were: "But for us,—who believe in right reason, in the duty and possibility of extricating and elevating our best self, in the progress of humanity towards perfection,—for us the framework of society, that theatre on which this august drama has to unroll itself, is sacred."[88] From this side of Arnold we may proceed to Irving Babbitt.

We should observe first that Babbitt, under the influence of Oriental philosophy, had arrived at a position close to the idealism of Bradley and even to the subjective idealism of Pater. (As far back as Schopenhauer, the similarity be-

86. *Essays in Criticism*, p. 113.
87. *Ibid.* Cf. the passage from "Isolation" Eliot quoted on page 107 of *The Use of Poetry:*

> And love, if love, of happier men.
> Of happier men, for they, at least,
> Have *dreamed* two human hearts might blend
> In one, and were through faith released
> From isolation without end
> Prolonged, nor knew, although no less
> Alone than thou, their loneliness.

88. Pp. 202–3.

tween subjective idealism and the Indian doctrine of Maya had been recognized.[89])Babbitt said:

> Man is cut off from immediate contact with anything abiding and therefore worthy to be called real and condemned to live in an element of fiction or illusion, but he may, I have tried to show, lay hold with the aid of the imagination on the element of oneness that is inextricably blended with the manifoldness and change and to just that extent may build up a sound model for imitation. One tends to be an individualist with true standards, to put the matter somewhat differently, only in so far as one understands the relation between appearance and reality —what the philosophers call the epistemological problem. This problem, though it cannot be solved abstractly and metaphysically, can be solved practically and in terms of actual conduct.[90]

In the last sentence we observe the reason for the strong moralistic bias in Babbitt. Having rejected "superstition," Babbitt is left with two positions to reconcile: individualism and social authority. His solution is to allow for the authority of the individual in *thought* (though he does not, of course, favor individualism for its own sake), and, to compensate, he stresses social authority in *conduct.* (This is much the same solution Arnold arrived at: "And how is criticism to show disinterestedness? By keeping aloof from practice; by resolutely following the law of its own nature, which is to be a free play of the mind on all subjects which it touches."[91])

I shall comment briefly on the political and social implications of Humanism before turning to its implications for literary criticism. In the essay "The Humanism of Irving Babbitt" Eliot pointed out the same irony that he found in Arnold: Babbitt based a doctrine of anti-individualism on

89. Copleston, *A History of Philosophy* (Part 2), 7: 33.
90. *Rousseau and Romanticism* (Cleveland: World Publishing Company, 1955), pp. 8–9.
91. "The Function of Criticism," *Essays in Criticism,* p. 20.

individualism: "If I have interpreted him correctly, he is thus trying to build a Catholic platform out of Protestant planks."[92] And so he feels in the end that Babbitt is "nearer to the view of Rousseau than . . . to the religious view."[93] Yet, when Eliot states his own idea of the relation of humanism and religion, we find exactly the same ambiguity as in Arnold and Babbitt (to clear up the ambiguity we have to turn back, as suggested above, to the analysis of the problem in the seventeenth and eighteenth centuries). Dogmatism *does* lead to individualism, and sceptical humanism to social solidarity, as well as vice-versa. As Eliot put it, "Humanism makes for breadth, tolerance, equilibrium and sanity. It operates against fanaticism. The world cannot get on without breadth, tolerance and sanity; any more than it can get on without narrowness, bigotry and fanaticism. "[94]

However, I cannot help but feel that Eliot's criticism of Humanism becomes telling when he turns to its hope of supplying *in practice* the place of religion, of influencing directly the behavior of more than a small fraction of mankind:

> I admit that all humanists—as humanists—have been individualists. As humanists, they have had nothing to offer to the mob. But they have usually left a place, not only for the mob, but (what is more important) for the mob part of the mind in themselves. Mr. Babbitt is too rigorous and conscientious a Protestant to do that: hence there seems to be a gap between his own individualism (and indeed intellectualism, beyond a certain point, must be individualistic) and his genuine desire to offer something which will be useful to the American nation primarily and to civilization itself.[95]

92. "The Humanism of Irving Babbitt," *Selected Essays*, pp. 423–24.
93. "Second Thoughts about Humanism," *Selected Essays*, p. 437.
94. *Ibid.*, p. 436.
95. "The Humanism of Irving Babbitt," *Selected Essays*, pp. 422–23.

Now let us turn to the effect on Arnold's and on Babbitt's critical taste of substituting literature for religion. Arnold's hope that poetry could supply the place of religion definitely determined what he looked for above all in poetry. "It is this chiefly [i.e., 'high seriousness']," he says, "which gives to our spirits what they can rest upon; and with the increasing demands of our modern ages upon poetry, this virtue of giving us what we can rest upon will be more and more highly esteemed."[96] Eliot was probably referring to this idea when he wrote of Arnold, "The same weakness, the same necessity for something to depend upon, which make him an academic poet make him an academic critic."[97]) Such demands on poetry are obviously going to affect—"distort" may in fact be the correct word—one's general system of critical valuations. But I am far from certain that such a critical program may not offer certain advantages as well as dangers. I do not think that Eliot was quite fair in saying that Arnold's criticism is "academic," that it is "an educator's view," that it is "tinged by . . . his own view of what it was best that his own time should believe."[98] The quality that Arnold was looking for was "the high seriousness which comes from absolute sincerity."[99] He gives these words substance by distinguishing acutely both Burns's "bravado" and his "preaching" from "the man speaking to us with his real voice." He finds that Burns's "genuine criticism of life, when the sheer poet in him speaks, is ironic."[100] It is my impression that the "consolation" that Arnold looks for in poetry is not so much the consolation *of* optimism as it is the consolation *for* pessimism, for having "seen things as they really are." It is notable that many of Arnold's touchstones are of a melan-

96. "The Study of Poetry," *Essays in Criticism,* p. 249.
97. *The Use of Poetry,* p. 108.
98. *Ibid.,* pp. 118, 110.
99. "The Study of Poetry," *Essays in Criticism,* p. 256.
100. *Ibid.,* pp. 255, 257.

choly or stoical tone, especially the ones from Homer, Dante, and Shakespeare that he quotes in "Byron."

It is in Babbitt that we find true didactic criticism. As Eliot explained it, "The trouble is that, for a modern humanist, literature thus becomes itself merely a means of approach to something else."[101] With little resistance Babbitt fell into the trap that posing a conflict between classicism and romanticism was bound to lay for him. When attempting to depreciate one kind of literature, you must set up an ideal against which to measure it, and be very careful in choosing this ideal, lest it discredit your program. Therefore, you put yourself in the position not only of throwing cold water on the enjoyment of the Romantic poets but also of having to say over and over again, tediously, that Dryden and Pope do not measure up to the classical ideal. However much you protest that it is *not* what you are doing, you are almost sure to fall into something in a way worse than the most frigid neoclassicism or the most doctrinaire romanticism. Thus Babbitt is likely to alienate everyone, and indeed from the point of view of the student of literature, Babbitt's was a depressing and thankless task. He was definitely not interested in literature primarily as literature.

Babbitt is like Ezra Pound at least in this, that he is left with a very scanty list of approved poets. In fact, the search for exemplars of some ideal or other and the consequent dissatisfaction with most existing poets is a weakness widespread in twentieth-century criticism. (This is due in part, no doubt, to what Eliot diagnosed as the impulse, conscious or not, to make of poetry a substitute for religion.) It is a sign of Eliot's good sense that, though somewhat liable to this heresy himself in his early criticism, he progressively rid himself of it. He seems to have escaped this heresy by reasoning thus: "In reviewing English po-

101. "Second Thoughts about Humanism," *Selected Essays*, p. 433.

etry, Mr. Read seems to charge himself with the task of casting out devils—though less drastically than Mr. Pound, who leaves nothing but a room well swept and not garnished. . . . If the malady is as chronic as that, it is pretty well beyond cure."[102]

But it would be an error to assume that Babbitt's significance for Eliot was ever as a literary critic. In 1959 Eliot recalled that "the one poem that Babbitt always held up for admiration was Gray's *Elegy*. And that's a fine poem but I think this shows certain limitations on Babbitt's part, God bless him."[103] In fact, I suspect that Eliot's gratitude to Babbitt was in part due to Babbitt's having done the dirty work that he himself might otherwise have been tempted to do and his having demonstrated the dangers of such work. I do not think it paradoxical to say that Babbitt's very rigidity could in this way have made possible Eliot's incomparably greater flexibility. But I certainly do not propose to explain away in such niggardly terms the unfailing loyalty to the memory of Babbitt that Eliot always expressed. In the first place, the relationship of Eliot to Babbitt just suggested presupposes Eliot's agreement with much of Babbitt's ethical position. In terms of the positions outlined in this introduction, Babbitt can be seen as opposing the impressionism and the subjectivism of Pater. If Eliot played Socrates to Pater's Protagoras, then we may see Babbitt as Parmenides.

But in his conception of the function of literature, Eliot is really no closer to the didacticism of Babbitt than to the aestheticism of Pater. Eliot's most telling criticism of Pater is not a denial of his doctrine of art for art's sake but a turning of Pater's own doctrine against him: "His famous dictum . . . is itself a theory of ethics; it is concerned not

102. *The Use of Poetry*, pp. 84–85.
103. "T. S. Eliot: The Art of Poetry" [an interview], *The Paris Review* 21 (Spring/Summer 1959): 49.

with art but with life." "Being primarily a moralist, he was
incapable of seeing any work of art simply as it is."[104] It was
perhaps in part through the help of Bradley that Eliot
found a way of asserting the integrity of literature and
describing its relation to religion, ethics, sociology, and
psychology without either subordinating it to, or making it
a substitute for, any of these. I shall defer a detailed analysis
of this topic to the chapter "Form," here only recalling my
previous reference to a gradual but fundamental change in
Eliot's critical vocabulary, a change that obscures the final
result, if there was one, of his attempt to wrestle with Romantic aesthetics and its idealist epistemology, and with
"the old *aporia* of Authority *v.* Individual Judgment." If
Eliot succeeded in getting beyond nineteenth-century criticism it was not so much by solving the problems it had
raised as by cultivating the spirit of earlier criticism: "This
criticism recognized literature as literature, and not as another thing. Literature was something distinct from philosophy and psychology and every other study. . . . I think we
should return again and again to the critical writings of the
seventeenth and eighteenth centuries, to remind ourselves
of that simple truth that literature is primarily literature, a
means of refined and intellectual pleasure."[105]

104. "Arnold and Pater," *Selected Essays,* pp. 389–90, 391.
105. "Experiment in Criticism," *The Bookman* 70 (November 1929): 226–27.

2
Eliot's Thesis: The Concept of the Point of View

Of the various ways of stating the idealist position, the one that can be made most plausible to common sense is a version of Zeno's paradox: the idealist questions the actual existence of the world's past, of even an instant ago. Here Bradley attacks realism: "The doctrine [that reality is 'the world of actual fact, and outside of this world floats the unsubstantial realm of the imaginary'] is in trouble at once with regard to the actual existence of past and future."[1] Even if it rejected in the end most of the idealist's conclusions, common sense might, by reflecting upon the idealist's question, realize that what we ordinarily think of as the world is to a great extent sustained in what we might call the "imagination," what Coleridge called the "primary imagination." Coleridge held "the primary IMAGINATION . . . to be the living Power and prime Agent of all human Perception, and as a repetition in the finite mind of the eternal act of creation in the infinite I AM."[2] Coleridge was probably influenced by Kant's theory of the function of the

1. *Essays on Truth and Reality* (Oxford: Clarendon Press, 1914), p. 30. See also p. 426.
2. *Biographia Literaria* (chapt. 13) in *Selected Poetry and Prose of Coleridge*, ed. Donald A. Stauffer (New York: Random House, 1951), p. 263.

59

imagination, a simple and concrete instance of which we may examine. Kant noticed that the imagination "completes the necessarily fragmentary data of the senses: it is impossible to perceive the *whole* of an object at once, yet we are seldom aware of the partial nature of our perception. For example, we cannot see more than three sides of a cube at one time, but we think of it as having all six sides."[3] Furthermore, the cube (or any other apparently discrete object), even as completed by the imagination, would be quite meaningless to us if isolated from its immediate surroundings, and these surroundings, in turn, would be meaningless except as part of a yet larger background—in the end, nothing short of a whole world achieves self-subsistence and thus meaning. But it is obvious that such a world can never be presented to us at once. For Kant, then, the imagination is a "blind but indispensable function of the soul, without which we should have no knowledge whatsoever, but of which we are scarcely ever conscious."[4]

In other words, it is the strategy of the type of idealist exemplified by Bradley and Eliot to present himself as a reluctant idealist. He agrees with the realist to find the "real" in that which is free from the "infection" of ideality, in what is prior to and independent of reflection, of the manipulation of the mind. He agrees, in short, that the ideal is "appearance" and not "reality." Furthermore, the idealist of this type agrees with at least some realists to locate the real in the immediate data of the senses, presented in the "here and now," the present instant. Having reached this point, however, the idealist observes how far we have gotten from what anyone (except a realist philosopher, driven to it by his doctrine) would consider reality. We have an insoluble dilemma. On the one hand, the whole

3. A. B. Manser, "Imagination," *The Encyclopedia of Philosophy*, 4:136. I quote Manser's exposition of Kant's concept.
4. *The Critique of Pure Reason*, quoted by Manser in *ibid.*

world that is the necessary background of any particular act of knowledge cannot be real; transcending the present moment, it is an "ideal construction," as Bradley calls it. On the other hand, "the moment isolated, with no before and after" cannot be real either; it is not only that it is meaningless; it does not exist. Any apparently discrete sensation is actually determined in part by the ideal world into which it must fit. As Eliot put it, "The idea, from one point of view apart from the world and attached to it, yet contains already the character of the world, a world . . . which shows by the very fact that that idea can be attached to it that it is somehow prepared for the reception of that idea."[5] (Compare with this the passage from the *Meno* quoted at the beginning of chapter 1.) Bradley's idealism, then, may be regarded as following from this proposition: that the past and the future have no existence apart from the present but that the present is what it is because of the past and the future.

Bradley's conception of the world as an ideal construction built up of the fragmentary data of the present instant may be compared with the conception set forth by Pater in the second paragraph of the "Conclusion" to *The Renaissance*. What Coleridge calls the primary imagination and Pater *a dream of a world*, Bradley calls a *finite centre*. Eliot, in his thesis and in his early criticism, uses the alternate terms *point of view* and *world*, as in his remark that "Mr. Conrad has no ideas, but he has a point of view, a 'world.' "[6] Eliot used these alternate terms because the first suggests subjective idealism and the second materialism, while Eliot's position is exactly midway between these: experience itself, rather than either subject or object, is reality. Eliot (following Bradley) would not allow any term like Coleridge's *imagination*, which suggests that some function on the sub-

5. *Knowledge and Experience* (New York: Farrar, Straus and Company, 1964), p. 39.
6. "Kipling Redivivus," *The Athenaeum* (May 9, 1919), p. 298.

ject side of experience is an irreducible principle. As Eliot put it, "The world is a construction. Not to say that it is *my* construction, for in that way 'I' am as much 'my' construction as the world is; but to use the word as best we can without implying any active agent: the world is a construction out of finite centres."[7]

Of course, *worlds* is more appropriate than *the world,* for there will be as many worlds as there are points of view. We must not, in fact, limit the number of these worlds to the human realm only: "The sea-anemone which accepts or rejects a proffered morsel is thereby relating an idea to the sea-anemone's world."[8] Furthermore, it would be erroneous to think of any individual as possessing one static world. The past sensations, like the past monuments of art, "form an ideal order among themselves, which is modified by the introduction of the new (the really new)."[9]

Eliot's thesis is based on what he calls "the doctrine of points of view."[10] Eliot's fundamental proposition is this: "My mind . . . I must treat as . . . absolute, in that it is a point of view from which I cannot possibly escape (to which indeed I am bound so closely that the word escape is without meaning)."[11] In the central portion of the thesis Eliot asserts the absoluteness of the individual point of view against its neglect by two recently developed "sciences." In chapter 3 he criticized the attempt of a school of psychology to separate the subjective aspect of any experience from the objective aspect so as to make of the former a set of objects to be studied by psychology. In chapters 4 and 5 Eliot criticized the attempt of the epistemologist, particu-

7. *Knowledge and Experience,* p. 166.
8. *Ibid.,* p. 44.
9. "Tradition and the Individual Talent," *The Sacred Wood,* 2nd ed. (London: Methuen, 1960), p. 50, and *Selected Essays,* 2nd ed. (New York: Harcourt, Brace and World, 1960), p. 5.
10. *Knowledge and Experience,* p. 90.
11. *Ibid.,* p. 145.

larly of the neorealist school, to define knowledge as the correspondence of ideas and judgments existing in the mind, with "facts" existing in a real world external to and independent of the mind.

To understand Eliot's objections to the method of the psychologists, one should first note that he did not object to behaviorism, as a psychological method. The behaviorist regards his subject from a purely "external" point of view, making no assumptions about what is going on in the "mind" of the subject and, indeed, no assumption as to the existence of that mind. According to Eliot, this is a valid point of view, but it is not the only one. There is the purely "internal" point of view, that of the subject himself, his attention directed, without self-consciousness, onto his object. The psychologist can only recognize the existence of this point of view; he cannot in any way *take* it. In the school that Eliot criticized, "the psychologist's error [is] treating two points of view as if they were one."[12] G. F. Stout, for example, defined *three* points of view operative when the psychologist observes a man enjoying a cigar: "1. The cigar known to the smoker. 2. The (cigar known to the smoker) as known to the psychologist. 3. The cigar known to the psychologist, in the role of private citizen."[13] Eliot insists that this second point of view simply does not exist, except as an illusion. Here we can perceive the principle that Eliot is applying: Bradley's doctrine that *any point of view is absolutely impenetrable by another point of view.*

It is only by confusing the external and the internal points of view that the psychologist persuades himself that he is able to identify and isolate "mental" phenomena: contents of consciousness (the collective term for ideas, images, presentations, etc.) and acts of the mind, such as will. Eliot asks, "For whom will my feeling be subjective?

12. *Ibid.*, p. 93.
13. *Ibid.*, p. 64.

For the dispassionate observer, who seeing the same object without the same feeling, subtracts my feeling from the object, to make of it a separate and independent entity existing in my mind."[14] But Eliot protests against this "arbitrary neglect of the individual": "The presentation, I shall argue, is identical with the object from the point of view of the experiencing subject, and from this point of view you have, in metaphysics, no appeal." "For so far as [things] are known to an individual mind they *are* simply, and that's an end of it."[15]

The psychologist's error is only one instance of what Eliot calls "the social point of view." Though a necessary point of view, it may at its worst, by encouraging the facile assumption that we understand the feelings of others (and of ourselves), result in the neglect of the only reality that feelings have—their reality for an individual point of view —and in the substitution for them of unreal abstractions. Eliot was later to observe that "Massinger dealt not with emotions so much as with the social abstractions of emotions."[16] In 1917 he wrote a curious dialogue, "Eeldrop and Appleplex." Eeldrop (not to be simply identified with Eliot, of course) remarks:

> With the decline of orthodox theology and its admirable theory of the soul, the unique importance of events has vanished. A man is only important as he is classed. Hence there is no tragedy, or no appreciation of tragedy, which is the same thing. We had been talking of young Bistwick, who three months ago married his mother's housemaid and now is aware of the fact. Who appreciates the truth of the matter? Not the relatives. . . . Not the generous minded and thoughtful outsider, who regards it merely as evidence for the necessity of divorce law reform. Bistwick is classed among the unhappily married. But what Bistwick feels when he wakes up in the morning, which is

14. *Ibid.*, p. 24.
15. *Ibid.*, pp. 61, 64.
16. "Philip Massinger," *The Sacred Wood*, p. 136, and *Selected Essays*, p. 190.

the great important fact, no detached outsider conceives. The awful importance of the ruin of a life is overlooked. . . . The majority of mankind live on paper currency: they use terms which are merely good for so much reality, they never see actual coinage."[17]

This passage takes on heightened interest, and even poignancy, when we realize, as I shall show in chapter 5 below, that when he wrote it, Eliot was also engaged, in his philosophical and in his critical writings, in a destructive analysis of the orthodox theory of the soul.

There is another interesting implication of the absoluteness, the impentrability of the individual point of view. For it follows that the point of view of the individual when *directed upon its objects* is impenetrable by the point of view of detached observer that the individual himself takes in introspection or self-consciousness. According to Eliot, "the movement between one 'finite centre' and another will not differ in kind from that inside of one consciousness."[18] Observe particularly the last clause of the following passage: "From a purely external point of view there is no will; and to find will in any phenomenon requires a certain empathy; we observe a man's actions and place ourselves partly but not wholly in his position; or we act, and place ourselves partly in the position of an outsider."[19] The self that experiences is not the same as the self that interprets the experience. Eliot insists, "The *I* who saw the ghost is not the *I* who had the attack of indigestion."[20] (This is part of an argument that the ghost cannot simply be dismissed as "unreal.") Thus Eliot is able to make a statement *apparently* at odds with his critique of the psychologist: "My emotions may be better understood by others than by my-

17. "Eeldrop and Appleplex, I," *The Little Review* 4 (May 1917): 9–10.
18. *Knowledge and Experience,* p. 91.
19. *Ibid.,* p. 81.
20. *Ibid.,* p. 121.

self; as my oculist knows my eyes."[21] The reader will have observed the connection between this attempt at a destructive analysis of self-consciousness and the irony of Eliot's early poetry. In 1933 Eliot mentioned, among the proper uses of irony, its "use (as by Jules Laforgue) to express a *dédoublement* of the personality *against which the subject struggles.*"[22] This problem of self-consciousness I shall return to later.

The psychologist's attempt to study the "contents of consciousness" as separate from objects rests upon an illusion, a confusion of two valid points of view. Mind itself exists only from the psychological point of view; in reality there is no mind substantial enough to "contain" ideas, but simply a *point* of view: "Mr. Conrad has no ideas, but he has a point of view, a 'world.' " There is, in short, nothing "inside" the point of view-world. Let us next examine Eliot's argument that there is nothing "outside" the point of view, either, except other points of view.

In chapters 4 and 5 Eliot argues, in opposition to the neorealist epistemologist (such as Bertrand Russell or G. E. Moore), that the individual point of view can never be measured against an external "real" world, independent of that point of view, so as to explain how it comes to know that world and to judge how closely its "ideas" correspond to that world. Eliot's primary method of argument is simply to insist again and again on the inherent self-contradiction of dualistic realism: "And these difficulties of a dualistic realism come from the standpoint of epistemology—of assuming that there is a real world *outside of our knowledge* and asking how we may *know* it."[23] This argument is intuitive rather than discursive; thus there is little more that can be said about it directly. But we can note that Eliot was fond

21. "Leibniz' Monads and Bradley's Finite Centres," in *ibid.,* p. 204.
22. "A Commentary," *The Criterion* 12 (April 1933): 469. (Latter italics mine.)
23. *Knowledge and Experience,* p. 109. (Italics mine.)

of pointing out how closely the neorealist came, paradoxically, to the position of Kant.

Eliot's criticism of the neorealist's real world is analogous to Bradley's arguments against Kant's "things in
themselves." The idea that we know of the existence of
unknowable "things in themselves" brings out a vein of
pleasantry in Bradley: "It would be much as if we said,
'Since all my faculties are totally confined to my garden, I
cannot tell if the roses next door are in flower.' "[24] Bradley
could not object to a theory that allowed us only partial
knowledge; he insists, in fact, that our knowledge cannot be
more than partial. But the result of the doctrine of "things
in themselves" is much more radical than this, according to
Bradley: "For it does not teach that our knowledge of reality is imperfect; it asserts that it does not exist. . . . There
is a hard and fast line, with our apprehension on one side
and the Thing on the other, and the two are hopelessly
apart."[25] Bradley's point is that if you define the real as that
which is independent of our knowledge, you are bound to
end in the position that we can know, not reality, but only
our "ideas" of it. Realism, which begins with the motive of
asserting our knowledge of a real world, ends, if it is hon-
est, with the denial that it is possible. As Eliot put it, "The
more closely one scrutinizes the 'external world,' and the
more eagerly and positively one plucks at it, the less there
is to see and touch."[26]

The purpose of chapter 2 of Eliot's thesis is to prove that
we cannot in the end draw a metaphysically valid distinction between the "real" and the "ideal" (he does not deny
that the distinction is necessary *in practice*). In other words,
it is a destructive analysis of the representational theory of

24. *Appearance and Reality*, 2nd ed. (Oxford: Clarendon Press, 1930), p. 111. For
Eliot's likening of the neorealists' position to that of Kant, see *Knowledge and
Experience*, p. 107.
25. *Appearance and Reality*, p. 111.
26. *Knowledge and Experience*, pp. 153–54.

knowledge, the theory that we can know only our own ideas of reality and not reality itself. Indeed, this is virtually the purpose of the whole thesis. We have seen that, in chapter 3, Eliot argued that ideas exist only from the psychological point of view, an illusion resulting from the confusion of the external and the internal points of view. We have already observed that the beginning and end of Bradley's philosophical endeavor is to overcome the total scepticism inherent in the representational theory. Paradoxical as it may seem, the doctrine that we cannot possibly escape from our points of view is aimed at asserting that we do have real, if imperfect, knowledge. Eliot clearly pointed to this purpose of his assertion of the absoluteness of the individual point of view: "A world which is built up from the subject's point of view [is], for the subject, . . . the only world, but it is not a solipsistic world, for it is not contrasted with any other possible world."[27] It is realism, according to which our knowledge *means to be something other than itself,* which ends in solipsism.

For Eliot, as for Bradley, real knowledge can be nothing short of the identity of the knowing and the known: immediate experience. This is the topic of chapter 1 of Eliot's thesis. And here is another paradox: knowledge is the beginning as well as the end of our search for knowledge (compare the paradox of the *Meno*). For you cannot start with subject and object and put them together to get knowledge: "If we attempt to put the world together again, after having divided it into consciousness and objects, we are condemned to failure. We cannot create experience out of entities which are independent of experience."[28] If, we may well ask, knowledge is the beginning, then whatever is the *end* of our search? The answer is—recognition: "the end of all our exploring / Will be to arrive where we started / And know the place for the first time."

27. *Ibid.*, p. 44.
28. *Ibid.*, p. 30.

The paradox results from the fact that we cannot, by definition, be directly conscious of immediate experience. It is important to note that Eliot does not justify the concept of immediate experience by appealing to an intuitive awareness of it, but by arguing that it is the only possible explanation of knowledge.[29] However, he does observe that, if "we did not think that at some moments our consciousness is nearer to 'pure' experience than at others," the concept would be quite useless.[30]

This concept of the "form" of knowledge, according to which knowledge *precedes* the development of self-consciousness (and, thus, consciousness of "objects"), applies at various levels of analysis. In the history of the human race, we can recognize the existence of the primitive or prephilosophical mind; "it is metaphysics which has produced the self."[31] But to stop there would be to sanction a primitivism to which Eliot does not subscribe. For we can recognize analogous stages and analogous development in the history of the individual. Furthermore, the same form of knowledge applies to each act of knowledge in the adult mind: "We stand before a beautiful painting, and if we are sufficiently carried away, our feeling [i.e., immediate experience] is a whole which is not, in a sense, *our* feeling, since the painting, which is an object independent of us, is quite as truly a constitutent as our consciousness or our soul. The feeling is neither here nor anywhere. . . . But in order that it should be feeling at all, it must be conscious, but so far as it is conscious it ceases to be merely feeling."[32] (The last sentence is a good statement of the paradox of immediate experience and consciousness.) Consequently, so far as

29. "Although we cannot know immediate experience directly as an object, we can yet arrive at it by inference, and even conclude that it is the starting point of our knowing, since it is only in immediate experience that knowledge and its object are one." *Knowledge and Experience*, p. 19.
30. *Ibid.*, pp. 17–18.
31. *Ibid.*, p. 155.
32. *Ibid.*, p. 20.

the theory of knowledge is concerned, "study of primitive consciousness seems futile; for we find in our own knowing exactly the same constitutents, in a clearer and more apprehensible form."[33] As Eliot put it in 1919: "The artist is, in an impersonal sense, the most conscious of men; he is therefore the most and the least civilized and civilizable; he is the most competent to understand both civilized and primitive. . . . He is the last person to see the savage in a romantic light, or to yield to the weak credulity of crediting the savage with any gifts of mystical insight or artistic feeling that he does not possess himself."[34]

The last step in Eliot's argument—the denial of the existence of things in themselves, or to put it more bluntly, of an external world independent of our knowledge of it—has perhaps imposed a severe strain on the credulity of the reader, a strain that I would willingly mitigate. Therefore, it is well to point out that Eliot presents it as a metaphysical truth with little direct effect on practical life. In fact, Eliot probably did not *believe* his denial of the existence of an external world in any simple sense of the word *believe*. In 1927 he wrote, "The poet makes poetry, the metaphysician makes metaphysics, the bee makes honey, the spider secretes a filament; you can hardly say that any of these agents believes: he merely does."[35] Furthermore, the main conclusions of the thesis are more or less independent of this last step in the argument; certainly this is true so far as the implications of the doctrine are relevant to a study of Eliot's criticism.

The assertion of the absoluteness of the individual point of view consists of two propositions. 1) Any point of view is impenetrable by another point of view, even when the two "belong" to the same self. With the possible exception

33. *Ibid.*, p. 17.
34. "War-Paint and Feathers," *The Athenaeum* (October 17, 1919), p. 1036.
35. "Shakespeare and the Stoicism of Seneca," *Selected Essays*, p. 118.

of the last clause, this proposition is not implausible; it even seems, upon reflection, obvious. 2) It is impossible to measure a point of view against an external real world independent of that point of view (we may agree to leave open the question of the *existence* of that world). I think that this proposition is plausible also. That it is a proposition acceptable to the contemporary scientist and even to the social scientist is demonstrated in a recent issue of *The New York Review of Books*.[36]

Now we may turn to a preliminary statement of the relevance of these propositions to Eliot's criticism. The concept of the impenetrability of the individual point of view leads directly to certain critical positions Eliot was later to take, such as, his rejection of "interpretation" (e.g., Coleridge or Goethe on Hamlet), his repeatedly expressed doubts about the significance of "communication" in literature, and his insistence that the "only way of expressing emotion in the form of art is by finding an 'objective correlative.' "[37] It is also evident that the emotional equivalent of this concept is often expressed in Eliot's poetry. The lines from *The Waste Land* annotated by the passage from Bradley are only the most striking example. The second proposition, which casts doubt on the accessibility of a real

36. "Physicists, novelists, logicians, and art historians have recognized for some time that what we call our knowledge of reality consists of images of it that we ourselves have fashioned. In the social sciences this is just now coming to be understood." Clifford Geertz, "In Search of North Africa," *The New York Review of Books* (April 22, 1971), p. 20.

"If we say that color and pitch are subjective, in virtue of their dependence on nervous systems or minds, consistency requires that we say the same of space, time and mass. . . . If a broad metaphysical distinction between "Appearance" and "Reality" is legitimate (it is not, in my opinion), there is just as much reason to place space and time in the category of Appearance as there is to place color and pitch there." C. Wade Savage, *The Measurement of Sensation*, quoted by D. W. Harding, "The Eyes Have It," *The New York Review of Books* (April 22, 1971), p. 40.

37. For Eliot's remarks about communication, see *The Use of Poetry*, 2nd ed. (London: Faber and Faber, 1964), pp. 27, 30, 115, 126, and 138.

world common to poet and audience, leads to Eliot's view that the work of art should be self-subsistent, in the sense that its meaning should not depend upon reference to "real life": "The closer a play is built upon real life, the more the performance by one actor will differ from another, and the more the performances of one generation of actors will differ from those of the next."[38] In fact, it would not be entirely facetious to say (paraphrasing Coleridge), grant me these two propositions, and I will cause the whole system of Eliot's critical theory to rise up before you.[39] This will be my task in subsequent chapters. At present, there is one more chapter of Eliot's thesis to be examined.

We have already considered the significance of the following statement: "My mind . . . I must treat as . . . absolute, in that it is a point of view from which I cannot possibly escape (to which indeed I am bound so closely that the word escape is without meaning)." The style in which this formulation of Eliot's position is expressed is probably a deliberate invitation to a charge that it amounts to solipsism. But in chapter 6 Eliot argued that the doctrine of points of view does not lead to solipsism. One reason for this we have already noted: "[His point of view], for the subject, is the only world, but it is not a solipsistic world, for it is not contrasted with any other possible world."[40] I do not suppose that we are meant to draw comfort from this disproof of solipsism, any more than from the other disproof, given in chapter 6.

The individual point of view would be solipsistic only if it were identical with, of if it depended upon, a self. But Eliot follows Bradley in denying that the self (or the soul or the ego or whatever term of similar import we wish to use) is real, that it is an essential or original element of

38. "Four Elizabethan Dramatists," *Selected Essays*, p. 96.
39. *Biographia Literaria* (chap. 13), p. 258.
40. *Knowledge and Experience*, p. 44.

experience. (It is just at this point that we can understand the motive behind the destructive analysis of the concept of personality in Eliot's early criticism. Our worlds are solipsistic if, and only if, the self is an irreducible principle.) In the opening pages of this chapter, I described Eliot's idealism as an absolutely rigorous application—a *reductio ad absurdum*—of realism. The only thing real, if to be real is to be independent of the operation of mind, is the experience of the present instant. Anything that transcends time is "ideal," is "constructed" from materials salvaged from the passing of the present instant. The self for Eliot is certainly (he quotes Bradley) such a "creature of an intellectual construction."[41] As such, the self takes its place among the other objects that go to make up the point of view. But this is somewhat too simple. If the self were merely an object, there would be nothing to bind together the points of view, which are, we must remember, the creatures of a moment, into a continuous whole.

If, in the world of appearance, we hypostatize the self, as to some extent we must, the self is subject as well as object. There are thus at least three entities recognized in Eliot's thesis that may be termed the self. At the level of reality, that is, of immediate experience, there is simply the *point* at which the contents of our world converge: As he expressed it in his famous analogy, "the mind of the poet is the shred of platinum."[42] If we ask, as Eliot did in an early philosophical essay, "Is personality equivalent to [the] totality of experience, or is it only a (very fiery) particle?" the answer is neither (or both), for the truth is exactly midway between.[43] In the world of conscious experience the self can be regarded in two different ways. We can take the

41. *Ibid.*, p. 150.
42. "Tradition and the Individual Talent," *The Sacred Wood*, p. 54, and *Selected Essays*, p. 7.
43. [Review of] *Religion and Science* by John Theodore Merz, *International Journal of Ethics* 27 (October 1916): 126.

external point of view, as does behaviorism, and regard the self as an object, as determined by its environment. Or we can take the internal view, as does subjective idealism, and regard the self as determining its world; this would be true solipsism. Eliot presents his position, so far as it can be explained at the level of conscious experience, as a mean that cannot be formulated between these two intelligible but unacceptable extremes: "Consciousness, we shall find, is reducible to relations between objects, and objects we shall find to be reducible to relations between different states of consciousness; and neither point of view is more nearly ultimate than the other. But if we attempt to put the world together again, after having divided it into consciousness and objects, we are condemned to failure. We cannot create experience out of entities which are independent of experience."[44] There is a striking return to these three concepts of the self thirty years after the completion of the thesis, in *The Cocktail Party:*

What is hell? Hell is oneself,
Hell is alone, the other figures in it
Merely projections.[45]

Or, take a surgical operation.
. . . .
In talking to the matron, you are still the subject,
The centre of reality. But, stretched on the table,
You are a piece of furniture in a repair shop.[46]

You must have learned how to look at people, Peter,
When you looked at them with an eye for the films:
That is, when you're not concerned with yourself
But just being an eye.[47]

44. *Knowledge and Experience*, p. 30.
45. *The Complete Poems and Plays, 1909–1950* (New York: Harcourt, Brace and World, 1962), p. 342.
46. *Ibid.*, p. 307.
47. *Ibid.*, p. 383.

I shall conclude this discussion of Eliot's thesis by pointing out that the position expounded there is remarkably like the one Coleridge set forth in the metaphysical chapters of *Biographia Literaria*. As to the difference—and in this difference we can perceive the essence of so much of Eliot's early criticism—it can be succinctly indicated in these sentences of Coleridge: "We are to seek therefore for some absolute truth capable of communicating to other positions a certainty, which it has not itself borrowed; a truth self-grounded, unconditional and known by its own light. . . . This principle . . . manifests itself in the SUM or I AM; which I shall hereafter indiscriminately express by the words spirit, self, and self-consciousness."[48] One consequence of Coleridge's confidence in the substantiality of the self is his belief that "the medium, by which spirits understand each other, is not the surrounding air; but the *freedom* which they possess in common."[49] In contrast, Eliot is certain that "we have no knowledge of other souls except through their bodies, because it is only thus that we can enter into their world."[50] Therefore, for Eliot, "the only way of expressing emotion in the form of art is by finding an 'objective correlative.' "

48. *Biographia Literaria* (chap. 12, Theses III and VI), pp. 247–48.
49. *Ibid.*, p. 237.
50. *Knowledge and Experience*, p. 151.

3
Sensation and Thought: The Dissociation of Sensibility and the Objective Correlative

In the previous chapter we examined Eliot's concept of the point of view, a world that can be described as "constructed" (if we "use the word as best we can without implying any active agent") about a "point" from the fragmentary data of the present instant. In his early criticism Eliot seems to be saying that the poet's world, like the world of Aristotle, ought to be made, not of ideas, emotions, motives, souls, and things, but of matter and form (or, as Eliot usually put it, *sensation* and *thought*). Because of the complications of self-consciousness, however, many poets do not build as they ought: "In England ideas run wild and pasture on the emotions; instead of thinking with our feelings (a very different thing) we corrupt our feelings with ideas; we produce the political, the emotional idea, evading sensation and thought. . . . James in his novels is like the best French critics in maintaining a point of view, a view-point untouched by the parasite idea."[1] Occasionally Eliot pushed this "objectivity" to the verge of behaviorism: "A 'living'

1. "In Memory," *The Little Review* 5 (August 1918): 46.

character is not necessarily 'true to life.' It is a person whom we can see and hear, whether he be true or false to human nature as we know it. What the creator of character needs is not so much knowledge of motives as keen sensibility; the dramatist need not understand people; but he must be exceptionally aware of them."[2]

The reference to Aristotle is not casual. Eliot called him "a moral pilot of Europe" and appealed to him frequently in his early criticism.[3] It is my opinion that Eliot's thesis can be seen as an attempt to correct Bradley's position by bringing it closer to Aristotle. (We could put this the other way and say that Eliot was correcting Aristotle by bringing him closer to Bradley. Eliot explained the main flaw in Aristotle's philosophy by saying that "Aristotle is here betrayed by his representation theory [of truth]—the exact correspondence between constituents of propositions and constituents of things; although in other contexts he is an epistemological monist."[4]) Eliot's thesis was completed while he was "a pupil of Harold Joachim, the disciple of Bradley who was closest to the master. . . . To Harold Joachim I owe a great deal: the discipline of a close study of the Greek text of the *Posterior Analytics,* and, through his criticism of my weekly papers, an understanding of what I wanted to say and of how to say it."[5] And shortly after completing his thesis, Eliot in two essays pointed out the shortcomings of Leibniz's theory of the soul (and of Bradley's by implication, since Eliot found Bradley's finite centres essentially similar to Leibniz's monads), compared with Aristotle's theory of the soul.[6]

2. "Philip Massinger," *The Sacred Wood,* 2nd ed. (London: Methuen, 1960), p. 132, and *Selected Essays,* 2nd ed. (New York: Harcourt, Brace and World, 1960), p. 188.

3. "Euripides and Professor Murray," *The Sacred Wood,* p. 73.

4. "The Development of Leibniz' Monadism," in *Knowledge and Experience* (New York: Farrar, Straus and Company, 1964), p. 184.

5. "Preface," *Knowledge and Experience,* p. 9.

6. "The Development of Leibniz' Monadism," *The Monist* 26 (October 1916):

If many passages in Eliot's early criticism suggest that the basic functions of intellectual life are two, sensation and thought, it is probably because these are the last two functions of Aristotle's soul (the first, nutrition, is obviously irrelevant to Eliot's purpose). The exclusion of certain other functions is intentional; Aristotle's reduction of movement (including desires and emotions) to sensation suits perfectly Eliot's critical and philosophical purposes and amounts, if applied to literary criticism, to almost the same thing as the concept of the objective correlative.[7] "Not only all knowledge, but all feeling, is in perception," Eliot insisted in "The Perfect Critic" (it is no coincidence that Aristotle comes closest to the ideal of the perfect critic).[8] In his thesis, Eliot had asked, "Why should anger be any less objective than pain-sensation?"[9]

The importance that, in the early criticism, Eliot attributed to sensation can be explained as due to the influence of Bradley, as well as of Aristotle: "Souls do not influence each other, except through their bodies. And hence it is only by this way that they are able to communicate."[10] But Bradley did not stress sensation any further than he was forced to by his position. So far as we explain it by influence, it is to that of Gourmont that I should attribute the remarkable sensationalism of Eliot's early criticism. Gourmont was an empiricist in his theory of ideas, holding them to be based on images. A possible explanation of Eliot's concept of the undissociated sensibility would be that it thinks in images rather than with abstract ideas. Later poets, unlike Donne, "do not feel their thought as

534–56: reprinted as "Appendix I" of *Knowledge and Experience*, pp. 177–97, and "Leibniz' Monads and Bradley's Finite Centres," *The Monist* 26 (October 1916): 566–76: reprinted as "Appendix II" of *Knowledge and Experience*, pp. 198–207.

7. Sir David Ross, *Aristotle*, 5th ed. (London: Methuen, 1964), p. 146. See *De Anima*, Bk. III, chap. 10.

8. *The Sacred Wood*, p. 10.

9. *Knowledge and Experience*, p. 70.

10. *Appearance and Reality*, 2nd ed. (Oxford: Clarendon Press, 1930), p. 304.

immediately as the odour of a rose."[11] In 1918 when Eliot
carried sensationalism to the furthest possible point—"all
thought and all language is based ultimately upon a few
simple physical movements"—he appealed for support to
Gourmont's *Problème du style.*[12] But this last formula is probably closer to behaviorism than to empiricism. We have
observed that the position Eliot took in his thesis can be
understood as an attempt to fuse together behaviorism and
subjective idealism, giving a result rather like Spinozism. In
fact, it is in explaining why Eliot was not an empiricist that
we approach his concept of the dissociation of sensibility.

In his early criticism, Eliot did not speak of "thinking in
images" but rather of "sensuous thought, or of thinking
through the senses, or of the senses thinking."[13] I suppose
that in the heyday of Imagism this distinction is significant.
Thinking in images would be analogous to the representational theory of knowledge, a destructive analysis of which
is the main theme of Eliot's thesis. I believe that Eliot saw
the change in sensibility that occurred in the seventeenth
century as analogous to the rise of the representational
theory of knowledge in European philosophy. The timing
is right; the philosophical theory was introduced by Descartes.[14] Or we may go back a little further. Descartes was
influenced by the use of the word *idea* for an entity existing
in the mind, a use common in sixteenth-century French and
English, notably in Montaigne. Significantly, it was Bradley
who finally drove this meaning of *idea* from the vocabulary
of English philosophy.[15] I certainly do not suggest that the
philosophical doctrine is the cause of the dissociation of
sensibility; probably Eliot would explain both develop-

11. "The Metaphysical Poets," *Selected Essays*, p. 247.
12. "Studies in Contemporary Criticism," *The Egoist* 5 (October 1918): 114.
13. "Imperfect Critics," *The Sacred Wood*, p. 23.
14. Copleston, *A History of Philosophy* (Garden City, N.Y.: Doubleday and Company, 1963), 4: 135.
15. J. O. Urmson, "Ideas," *The Encyclopedia of Philosophy*, 4: 119–20.

ments as symptoms of causes operating at "a depth at
which words and concepts fail us," as he wrote in 1947.[16]
But I believe that Eliot thought of the unified sensibility as
becoming dissociated when the poet becomes self-conscious: when he becomes aware, that is, of his ideas, images, and feelings as distinct from the objects that caused
them. In this situation, his attention is *reflected* from the
object to the contents of his own mind. This is the meaning
that the word *reflection* has for Eliot: "The difference [is]
between the intellectual poet and the reflective poet. Tennyson and Browning are poets, and they think; but they do
not feel their thought as immediately as the odour of a
rose."[17] And again, "The sentimental age began early in
the eighteenth century, and continued. The poets . . .
thought and felt by fits, unbalanced; they reflected."[18]

In an essay of 1921 that has not been republished, Eliot
succeeded in formulating much more clearly than in the
familiar essays his concept of the dissociated sensibility.
The following passage from that essay is also valuable because it indicates that the search for the objective correlative is the remedy for the dissociation of sensibility.

The strongest, like Mr. Joyce, make their feeling into an articu-
late external world; what might crudely be called a more feminine type, when it is also a very sophisticated type, makes its
art by feeling and by contemplating the feeling, rather than the
object which has excited it or the object into which the feeling
might be made. Of this type of writing the recent book of
sketches by Mrs. Woolf, Monday or Tuesday, is the most extreme example. A good deal of the secret of the charm of Mrs.
Woolf's shorter pieces consists in the immense disparity between the object and the train of feeling which it has set in
motion. Mrs. Woolf gives you the minutest datum, and leads

16. "Milton II," *On Poetry and Poets* (New York: Farrar, Straus and Giroux,
1961), p. 173.
17. "The Metaphysical Poets," *Selected Essays*, p. 247.
18. *Ibid.*, p. 248.

you on to explore, quite consciously, the sequence of images and feelings which float away from it. The result is something which makes Walter Pater appear an unsophisticated rationalist, and the writing is often remarkable. The book is one of the most curious and interesting examples of a process of dissociation which in that direction, it would seem, cannot be exceeded.[19]

We must understand that the unified sensibility is an ideal limit rather than an actuality. Eliot pointed out in his thesis that only a "solitary autochthon" could be completely unconscious of his own ideas and feelings as distinct from their objects.[20] In social behavior—even in the most unified and "organic" society, supported by the most powerful orthodoxy—there is bound to be some conflict between points of view, so that we are aware that other persons have feelings about a given object different from ours and thus that our feelings are to some degree distinct from the object. (It is this situation, in fact, that gives rise to the belief in an "external" world and at the same time to the belief in a "self.") "It is only in social behaviour," Eliot remarked in his thesis, "in the conflict and readjustment of finite centres, that feelings and things are torn apart. And after this separation they leave dim and drifting edges, and tend to coalesce."[21] The "cure" for the dissociated sensibility is to pursue this tendency of feelings and objects to coalesce, to direct the attention *outward,* to search for an objective correlative of the feeling, "the object which has excited it or the object into which the feeling might be made."

Eliot never made a detailed and consistent application of the concept of the dissociation of sensibility to the history of English literature. I believe that this failure is in part due to his indecision as to the place of the Elizabethans and of Donne in the history of sensibility. In his earliest criticism,

19. "London Letter," *The Dial* 71 (August 1921): 216–17.
20. *Knowledge and Experience*, p. 37.
21. *Ibid.*, pp. 24–25.

of course, they are taken as models of the unified sensibility. Two possible explanations for the quality Eliot found in them may be inferred from his remarks. In one passage he seems to place them in the tradition of Dante, Guido Cavalcanti, Guinizelli, and Cino.[22] This may amount to saying that they possessed what is sometimes called today "the sacramental view of nature." But in "The Metaphysical Poets," there is a hint of another explanation, more consistent with Eliot's thought as a whole. Commenting on the high "degree of development of sensibility" in the later Elizabethan and early Jacobean poets, Eliot observes that "if we except Marlowe, a man of prodigious intelligence, these dramatists were directly or indirectly (it is at least a tenable theory) affected by Montaigne."[23] Eliot is suggesting, I believe, that the pyrrhonism of Montaigne dissolved, for these poets, the conventional world view they inherited and thus allowed them to build anew, allowed them "ériger en lois ses impressions personnelles."[24] It was to these poets that Eliot unfavorably compared Philip Massinger, "who, at the moment when a new view of life is wanted, . . . looked at life through the eyes of his predecessors."[25] This judgment is much the same as that in another comment about Massinger, that he "dealt not with emotions so much as with the social abstractions of emotions."[26]

If my interpretation of Eliot's remark about the influence of Montaigne is correct, it would help to explain Eliot's likening of the metaphysical poets to the French poets of the later nineteenth century.[27] For—at least it was Gourmont's theory—the philosophical basis of the Symbolist movement was subjective idealism, which would come to very much the same thing as Montaigne's pyrrhonism.

22. "The Metaphysical Poets," *Selected Essays*, p. 247.
23. *Ibid.*, p. 245.
24. "The Perfect Critic," *The Sacred Wood*, pp. 1, 5.
25. "Philip Massinger," *The Sacred Wood*, p. 143, and *Selected Essays*, p. 195.
26. *The Sacred Wood*, p. 136, and *Selected Essays*, p. 190.
27. "The Metaphysical Poets," *Selected Essays*, p. 249.

But it is likely that the distinction betwen the unified and the dissociated sensibility is a fine one. Pyrrhonism cuts both ways, against the "impersonal ideas which obscure what we really are and feel, what we really want, and what really excites our interest," but also against the personal point of view.[28] In a reassessment of the poet in 1931, Eliot found that "in Donne, there is a manifest fissure between thought and sensibility, a chasm which in his poetry he bridged in his own way, which was not the way of mediaeval poetry."[29] In the course of elaborating this interpretation of Donne, Eliot noted that "his attitude towards philosophic notions in his poetry may be put by saying that he was more interested in *ideas* themselves as objects than in the *truth* of ideas. In an odd way, he almost anticipates the philosopher of the coming age, Descartes." Then Eliot quoted a passage from the sixth Meditation in which Descartes asserts that it is only "with probability" that he can conjecture that bodies exist to correspond to his ideas.[30] Donne "was more interested in ideas themselves as objects than in the truth of ideas"—this is an exact analogy to the representational theory of knowledge in philosophy. Corresponding to this reassessment of Donne is the new interpretation of the Elizabethan and Jacobean dramatists that Eliot made in the late twenties: "What influence the work of Seneca and Machiavelli and Montaigne seems to me to exert in common on that time, and most conspicuously through Shakespeare, is an influence toward a kind of self-consciousness that is new; the self-consciousness and self-dramatization of the Shakespearean hero, of whom Hamlet is only one."[31] Eliot seems finally to have decided that the Elizabethan and Jacobean poets, like their successors, suffered a dissociation of sensibility.

28. "Blake," *The Sacred Wood*, p. 154, and *Selected Essays*, p. 277.
29. "Donne in Our Time," in *A Garland for John Donne*, ed. Theodore Spencer (Cambridge: Harvard University Press, 1931), p. 8.
30. *Ibid.*, p. 11.
31. "Shakespeare and the Stoicism of Seneca," *Selected Essays*, p. 119.

If the theory of the dissociation of sensibility was never successfully incorporated into Eliot's critical view as a whole, the concept of the objective correlative is almost the essence of that critical view, as I believe my discussion has demonstrated. (If the phrase itself did not survive as a part of Eliot's critical vocabulary, that is no doubt due to its being felt to be too "heavy" for polite criticism; it certainly sounds barbarous.) Having already devoted considerable space to analysis of this concept (see Objective correlative in Index), I shall pass on to consider "thought," after briefly showing the connection of the objective correlative with another main theme of Eliot's criticism.

In the course of explaining the superiority of Rostand to Maeterlinck, Eliot asserted that poetic drama "must take genuine and substantial human emotions, such emotions as observation can confirm, typical emotions."[32] Observe the similarity between this statement and the passage from the *Meno,* and the interplay of the meanings of the words *substantial* and *confirm.* In a philosophical essay written three years earlier, Eliot had remarked that "in general, for Aristotle as well as for Plato, whatever was merely individual was perishable and incapable of being a subject of knowledge. . . . For the Greek the human was the typically human, individual differences were not of scientific interest."[33] Eliot's emphasis on the objective correlative is a compensation for the extreme "subjectivity" of the notion of the point of view as impenetrable. We cannot escape from our points of view, but we can construct them only of "what observation can confirm." Interest in the purely personal emotion would be interest "as with Maeterlinck in the emotion which cannot be expressed."[34]

32. " 'Rhetoric' and the Poetic Drama," *The Sacred Wood,* p. 84, and *Selected Essays,* p. 29.
33. "The Development of Leibniz' Monadism," in *Knowledge and Experience,* pp. 185–86.
34. " 'Rhetoric' and the Poetic Drama," *The Sacred Wood,* p. 84, and *Selected Essays,* p. 29.

I turn now to consider the nature and the function of thought. We have seen so far that thought is not best conceived as the manipulation of "ideas," which are recognized only after the sensibility is dissociated, that is, after self-consciousness—a *confusion* of internal and external points of view—has separated the subjective from the objective. In fact, we can get at least a sketchy conception of Eliot's "thinking through the senses" from the essay "The Perfect Critic" and this essay again can be seen as an anticipation of the theory of the dissociation of sensibility.

"The Perfect Critic" suggests a method of thinking that is a mean between, or a synthesis of, or the undissociated form of, two heretical ways of thinking: the abstract—thought operating in (relative) independence of sensation—and the impressionistic—sensation operating in (relative) independence of organizing thought. Of the first of these heresies, I shall observe only that it is "reflective" in the sense defined above. Eliot suggested that its popularity was due in part to the influence of Hegel, whom he accused of "dealing with his emotions as if they were definite objects which had aroused those emotions."[35] More relevant to our present purpose is Eliot's criticism of the opposing method, which, he suggests, can be traced back at least as far as Pater: the impressionistic. The professed aim of the impressionistic critic is "to exhibit to us, like the plate, the faithful record of the impressions . . . upon a mind more sensitive than our own."[36]

Of this aim Eliot observed (choosing his verb carefully) that "you never rest at the pure feeling. . . . The moment you try to put the impressions into words, you either begin to analyse and construct, to 'ériger en lois,' or you begin to create something else."[37] We have noted above that the case against realism made by Bradley and Eliot derived its

35. "The Perfect Critic," *The Sacred Wood,* p. 9.
36. *Ibid.,* p. 3.
37. *Ibid.,* p. 5.

force from eliciting the reader's sense of the "meaningless-ness" of the isolated sensation. The pure impression would have meaning only if there were an organized external world to which it might be referred and if the organization of that world were readily accessible to all minds in common. Eliot and Bradley deny both of these conditions, but one may, for the sake of plausibility, understand their position as following from the denial of the second condition only. The poet, then, must not merely rely on an organization existing somewhere outside of the poem, in an external world or, we might add, in his own mind. He must get the organization out into the poem itself: "A variety of passages might illustrate the assertion that no emotion is contemplated by Dante purely in and for itself. . . . [It] is always preserved entire, but is modified by the position assigned . . . in the eternal scheme."[38]

Eliot concludes that "Dante helps us to provide a criticism of M. Valéry's 'modern poet' who attempts 'to produce in us a *state.*' A state, in itself, is nothing whatever."[39] For Eliot, the isolated impression is as insubstantial as the abstraction: "An impression needs to be constantly refreshed by new impressions in order that it may persist at all; it needs to take its place in a system of impressions."[40] As he expresses it in *Four Quartets:* "Not the intense moment / Isolated, with no before and after, / But a lifetime burning in every moment."

We have examined above Eliot's destructive analysis of the representational theory of knowledge and of the assumption on which it rests—that consciousness is substantial enough to have "contents": ideas, images, feelings, and the like. I believe that we may put the conception of thought and sensation assumed in Eliot's thesis and in his early criticism in this simple formula: *thought provides the form*

---

38. "Dante," *The Sacred Wood,* p. 167.
39. *Ibid.,* p. 170.
40. "The Perfect Critic," *The Sacred Wood,* p. 14.

only, not the matter, of our worlds (points of view); the matter is sensation. To be precise, we should say that this is the way in which thought and sensation *ought* to cooperate, rather than the way in which they always *do:* "In England ideas run wild and pasture on the emotions."

Eliot recognized two main categories of thought: logic (or "rational necessity") and association.[41] The first of these he prefers, though he does not dismiss the second. We may say that Eliot is concerned with *formal logic,* if by that we mean, not the use of the syllogism, but a logic that, as I suggested in the previous paragraph, provides the *form* of our knowledge. Logic as the poet knows it will of course be different from logic as the philosopher knows it. Eliot's formula for the former is "the logic of sensibility." Of the *Divine Comedy* he asserted, "Every degree of the feeling of humanity, from lowest to highest, has, moreover, an intimate relation to the next above and below, and all fit together according to the logic of sensibility."[42]

Eliot's concept of "the logic of sensibility" may have been suggested by a passage in *Essays on Truth and Reality* in which Bradley protests against the "incredible doctrine" that "thought is abstract, . . . while imagination is concrete." "In short," Bradley declared, "to set up imagination and thought as two separate faculties, and to speak of one using the other . . . is from first to last erroneous and indefensible. Imagination, if of a certain kind, is not something employed by thought, but is itself thinking proper. If, on the other hand, by mere imagination we mean our mental flow so far as that is subjected to no control whatever, and is so not 'used' at all, this certainly is not imagination in the higher sense of the word. Mere imagination, where regulated logically, itself is inference."[43]

Everywhere in Eliot's early criticism we meet such

---

41. For the phrase *rational necessity* see "Andrew Marvell," *The Nation & The Athenaeum* 33 (September 29, 1923): 809.
42. "Dante," *Selected Essays,* p. 229.
43. Pp. 364–65.

phrases as *a system of impressions, a system of perceptions and feelings, a system of feelings or of morals.* [44] Occasionally Eliot even used the word *logic,* as when he remarked of a poem of Jean de Bosschère, "I am not able to follow the development of these images into a logical structure." [45] With Dante it is otherwise: "Proceeding through the *Inferno* on a first reading, we get a succession of phantasmagoric but clear images, of images which are coherent, in that each reinforces the last." [46]

Such statements are an equivalent in literary criticism of a well-known philosophical doctrine that, in England, was formulated primarily by Bradley and by Harold Joachim, Bradley's disciple and Eliot's tutor: the coherence theory of truth. This theory was formulated in opposition to the "new realists," such as Bertrand Russell and G. E. Moore, who were trying to put idealism to flight by demonstrating that the truth of a judgment in our minds lay in its *correspondence* to a fact in the external world. The dualism inherent in this view was unacceptable to the idealists; not only was it fatal to idealism but it was, in fact, virtually a return to the representational theory of knowledge, though the new realists also had set themselves against that theory. Therefore, the idealists countered with the theory that "to say a statement (usually called a judgment) is true or false is to say that it coheres or fails to cohere with a system of other statements; that it is a member of a system whose elements are related to each other by ties of logical implication." [47] We may put Bradley's view briefly in this way: We assume that if we could take a complete view of reality, it would be seen to be ordered and consistent, though the part of real-

44. "The Perfect Critic," *The Sacred Wood,* p. 14; "The Education of Taste," *The Athenaeum* (June 27, 1919), p. 521; "Andrew Marvell," *Selected Essays,* p. 251.
45. "Reflections on Contemporary Poetry," *The Egoist* 4 (October 1917): p. 133.
46. "Dante," *Selected Essays,* p. 208.
47. *The Encyclopedia of Philosophy,* 2: 130.

ity within any one "finite centre" is inconsistent, as immediately perceived, because partial. And because the whole of reality must be consistent, we make a partial point of view not less but more true to the whole if we make consistent its immediate disorder, even if that is only possible by adopting a convention as to what is accepted as real and what is not.

The function of logic in providing the *structure* of the work of art as a whole will be examined further in the chapter "Form." Here we may analyze some remarks that Eliot made on the function of thought in the fabrication of the *texture* of the poem. He recognizes the operation, at this level of composition, of two main categories of thought: logic and association. True to his philosophical training, he places the higher value on logic, though he does not reject association—"there is much that is good in the logic of Mill and the psychology of Bain."[48]

The distinction between logic (or "rational necessity") and association corresponds to the distinction between metaphor and conceit: "In a conceit two things very different are brought together, and the spark of ecstacy generated in us is a perception of power in bringing them together."[49] Association is spontaneous; Eliot once glossed the word *inspiration* as "free association from the unconscious."[50] Defined not in terms of the mind of the poet but in terms of the quality it imparts to the poem, association is "suggestiveness."[51]

In the metaphor (Eliot had just quoted that favorite touchstone of his: "In her strong toil of grace"), "instead of contrast we have fusion: a restoration of language to

48. "Francis Herbert Bradley," *Selected Essays*, p. 398.
49. "Andrew Marvell," *The Nation & The Athenaeum* 33 (September 29, 1923): 809.
50. "Dryden the Critic, Defender of Sanity," *The Listener* 5 (April 29, 1931): 725.
51. "Andrew Marvell," *The Nation & The Athenaeum* 33 (September 29, 1923): 809.

contact with things."[52] Elsewhere he said of this same metaphor that it "identifies itself with what suggests it."[53] In other words, metaphor is an instance of the objective correlative; it brings together not two things but a feeling and an object, the only object that precisely expresses that feeling.

A further distinction between association and logic is that the first is personal while logic is universal. A case of association may depend upon a particular mind to give it meaning. Thus, Eliot later criticized his own collocation of Classicism, Catholicism, and Royalism: "That there are connexions for me I of course admit, but these illuminate my own mind rather than the external world."[54] On the other hand, Eliot remarked of the metaphor from *Antony and Cleopatra:* "Such words have the inevitability which make [*sic*] them appropriate to be spoken by any character."[55] Inevitability or "rational necessity" is, no doubt, the distinguishing mark of logic; an association that every mind must make would *be* logic.

The distinction between logic and association should correspond, I think, to that between the unified and the dissociated sensibility. Eliot explained that some poets, including himself, on occasion experienced a condition like "automatic writing" or "inspiration" in which was produced "an outburst of words which we hardly recognise as our own."[56] He gives as an example the collocation of images that Chapman borrowed from Seneca ("Fly where the evening," etc.) and that he himself borrowed in turn from Chapman: "I suggest that what gives it such intensity as it has in each case is its saturation—I will not say with

52. *Ibid.*
53. "Philip Massinger," *The Sacred Wood,* p. 128, and *Selected Essays,* p. 185.
54. *After Strange Gods* (New York: Harcourt, Brace and Company, 1934), p. 29.
55. "Andrew Marvell," *The Nation & The Athenaeum* 33 (September 29, 1923): 809.
56. *The Use of Poetry,* 2nd ed. (London: Faber and Faber, 1964), p. 145.

'associations,' for I do not want to revert to Hartley—but with feelings too obscure for the authors even to know quite what they were." ("Why, for all of us, out of all that we have heard, seen, felt, in a lifetime, do certain images recur, charged with emotion, rather than others?")[57] But Eliot warns that "I cannot think of Shakespeare or Dante as having been dependent upon such capricious releases."[58] The poet whose system of thought is congruent with his system of feeling, whether because he has elevated into laws his personal impressions or because he uses the idea that "has reached the point of immediate acceptance, . . . has become almost a physical modification," the poet who understands his feelings, has not two worlds, of feelings and of objects, which must be associated, but one world of feeling embodied in its objective correlative. Dryden had noticed the apparently spontaneous inevitability in the operation of Shakespeare's imagination: "All the images of nature were still present to him, and he drew them not laboriously, but luckily."[59] Shakespeare, we might say, had "no ideas, but he [had] a point of view, a 'world.' "[60]

The significance of metaphor for Eliot is due ultimately to his sense that it is not an occasional "poetic" device but the basic principle of *all* language that goes beyond direct physical description. Thus he rebuked an admirer of Meredith's "conceits": "Had he studied the history of language in his critical education he might have perceived finally that all thought and all language is based ultimately upon a few simple physical movements. Metaphor is not something applied externally for the adornment of style, it is the life of style, of language. If Mr. Crees had realized how completely we are dependent upon metaphor for even the ab-

57. *Ibid.*, pp. 147–48.
58. *Ibid.*, p. 146.
59. *Of Dramatic Poesy and Other Critical Essays*, ed. George Watson (New York: E. P. Dutton and Company, 1964), 1: 67.
60. "Kipling Redivivus," *The Athenaeum* (May 9, 1919), p. 298.

stractest thinking, he would admit . . . that the Carlyle-Meredith metaphor is excrescent."[61]

Eliot's distinction between logic and association is very like Coleridge's distinction between imagination and fancy, though Eliot often criticized Coleridge's distinction. But Eliot was not being inconsistent; it was not Coleridge's distinction but his degradation of association (fancy) to which Eliot objected.[62] For Eliot, in poetry at its best, not only is every word a metaphor, but every word is also a case of association.

> The music of a word is, so to speak, at a point of intersection: it arises from its relation first to the words immediately preceding and following it, and indefinitely to the rest of its context; and from another relation, that of its immediate meaning in that context to all the other meanings which it has had in other contexts, to its greater or less wealth of association. . . . At certain moments . . . a word can be made to insinuate the whole history of a language and a civilization. This is an 'allusiveness' which is not the fashion or eccentricity of a peculiar type of poetry; but an allusiveness which is in the nature of words.[63]

At the point of intersection the word expresses the immediate experience of the poet *and* "the mind of Europe"—"here, now, always."

I shall now draw together the material of this chapter and make several general conclusions about it. First, we may consider the motive for Eliot's remarkable emphasis on sensation and thought in his early criticism and for his reduction of emotion and feeling to perception. The primary reason for this emphasis is that sensation and thought, as against emotion and feeling, are *impersonal* and *universal*. The value of Dante's allegorical method is that it makes possible the use of clear visual images: "Speech

61. "Studies in Contemporary Criticsm," *The Egoist* 5 (October 1918): 114.
62. *The Use of Poetry*, pp. 29, 77–79.
63. "The Music of Poetry," *On Poetry and Poets*, pp. 25–26.

varies, but our eyes are all the same."[64] In contrast, Hegel dealt "with his emotions as if they were definite objects which had aroused those emotions. His followers have as a rule taken for granted that words have definite meanings, overlooking the tendency of words to become indefinite emotions."[65]

Sensation is not emphasized comparably in Eliot's later criticism, at least not explicitly. That theme is absorbed in a more general and more enduring one: the theme of "seeing the object as it really is." In the late criticism Eliot did not appear to conceive of "seeing the object" so insistently in terms of sensation as he had done earlier. But sensation does remain a necessary condition, I believe. As late as 1941 Eliot wrote that "the first condition of right thought is right sensation."[66] The great emphasis on sensation in the early criticism is probably due to a specific program: to oppose "the effort to construct a dream-world, which alters English poetry so greatly in the nineteenth century."[67] And this program is transcended or transformed in the later criticism.

64. "Dante," *Selected Essays,* p. 205.
65. "The Perfect Critic," *The Sacred Wood,* p. 9.
66. "Rudyard Kipling," *On Poetry and Poets,* p. 289.
67. "Andrew Marvell," *Selected Essays,* p. 259.

4
Self-Consciousness versus Looking at the Object

Self-consciousness was for Eliot a topic of peculiar interest and a problem of unusual difficulty. He devoted considerable attention to it in *The Use of Poetry*, beginning his chapter "The Modern Mind" with a quotation from Maritain about the "fearful progress in self-consciousness" in modern art. Some pages further on he remarked, "Whether the self-consciousness involved in aesthetics and in psychology does not risk violating the frontier of consciousness, is a question which I need not raise here; it is perhaps only my private eccentricity to believe that such researches are perilous if not guided by sound theology."[1] Six years later, he advised *poets* not to read even *Situation de la poésie,* in which Jacques and Raissa Maritain discussed the dangers of aesthetics and psychology.[2]

Eliot had a sharp eye for ordinary human self-consciousness and particularly for the insidious pleasures of what he called "self-dramatization." Here we may observe a striking change in his attitude. In 1919, in " 'Rhetoric' and Poetic Drama," he discussed self-dramatization with appar-

1. 2nd ed. (London: Faber and Faber, 1964), p. 150.
2. "A Commentary: That Poetry is Made with Words," *The New English Weekly* 15 (April 27, 1939): 27.

ent scientific objectivity, treating it on the one hand simply as a common human trait and on the other as a phenomenon "of very great usefulness to dramatic verse." One of the illustrations he chose in this essay was Othello's last speech: "The really fine rhetoric of Shakespeare occurs in situations where a character in the play *sees himself* in a dramatic light:

OTHELLO. And say, besides,—that in Aleppo once . . ."[3]

Eight years later Eliot again commented on the same passage, but with a noticeably altered tone: "What Othello seems to me to be doing in making this speech is *cheering himself up.* He is endeavouring to escape reality, he has ceased to think about Desdemona, and is thinking about himself. . . . I do not believe that any writer has ever exposed this *bovarysme,* the human will to see things as they are not, more clearly than Shakespeare." Othello "takes in the spectator"; whether he took in Shakespeare Eliot does not say, leaving it open whether Shakespeare was "illustrating, consciously or unconsciously, human nature."[4] The *idea* is almost the same as in the comment eight years before, but now Eliot raises so many moral questions that he in fact suggests a radically new interpretation of *Othello.* Moreover, he now takes the passage as a symptom of a peculiarly modern disease—"a kind of self-consciousness that is new"—caused in part by the combined influences of Seneca, Machiavelli, and Montaigne.[5]

Eliot's personal reaction to self-dramatization manifested itself pungently in an essay of 1933. Ridiculing the various kinds of pseudo-sophistication he found in modern literature (in America the current fashion "takes the form

3. *Selected Essays,* 2nd ed. (New York: Harcourt, Brace and World, 1960), p. 27.
4. *Ibid.,* p. 111.
5. *Ibid.,* p. 119.

of what they call hard boiling"), Eliot remarked pointedly, "If the Chinese bandits ever discover that they are hard boiled I shall have to infer that the oldest civilization in the world has reverted to the condition of puerility."[6]

Before turning to other kinds of self-consciousness, I should define the term. I am using the definition that emerged from the last chapter: *attention to one's ideas, images, feelings as entities distinct from their objects.* I believe that this definition indicates the common element in the various kinds of self-consciousness with which Eliot dealt.

Another kind of self-consciousness that occupied Eliot's attention from at least as early as the writing of his thesis until the end of his career is caused by theory that affects practice. In a lecture of 1948 he said, "In affecting writing, the theory becomes a different thing from what it was merely as an explanation of how the poet writes. And Valéry was a poet who wrote very consciously and deliberately indeed. . . . He was the most self-conscious of all poets."[7] So far as criticism is concerned, this kind of self-consciousness is to be avoided: "We can of course—and this is a danger to which the philosophical critic of art may be exposed—adopt a theory and then persuade ourselves that we like the works of art that fit into that theory. But I am sure that my own theorizing has been epiphenomenal of my tastes, and that in so far as it is valid, it springs from direct experience of those authors who have profoundly influenced my own writing."[8]

But Eliot saw that theory and practice can never be distinguished completely. As he put it in his thesis, "Practice, and this is the difficulty . . . is shot through with theory, and theory with practice."[9] Taking a broad historical view one

6. "A Commentary," *The Criterion* 12 (April 1933): 471.
7. *To Criticize the Critic* (New York: Farrar, Straus and Giroux, 1965), p. 39.
8. *Ibid.,* p. 20.
9. *Knowledge and Experience* (New York: Farrar, Straus and Company, 1964), p. 137.

can see that theory enters practice and profoundly alters the world: "As it is metaphysics which has produced the self so it is epistemology, we may say, which has produced knowledge. It is perhaps epistemology . . . that has given us the fine arts; for what was at first expression and behaviour may have developed under the complications of self-consciousness, as we became aware of ourselves as reacting aesthetically to the object."[10]

Eliot also considered concern with style, in the composition of poetry, as a kind of self-consciousness. In the lecture of 1948 "From Poe to Valéry," Eliot suggested that poetry tends to show a historical development from a primitive level of almost total concentration on subject matter to a late stage of great sophistication, at which style is the primary interest: "This process of increasing self-consciousness—or, we may say, of increasing consciousness of language—has as its theoretical goal what we may call *la poésie pure*. . . . The subject exists for the poem, not the poem for the subject."[11]

On occasion, Eliot reacted rather strongly against this "process of increasing self-consciousness." Of the prose writers of the latter half of the nineteenth century, he wrote, in 1935, "The stylists depart: Carlyle is too violent, Ruskin too unrestrained, Meredith too whimsical, Arnold appears conscious of his abilities to the verge of vulgarity. . . . Those writers remain who were more interested in their subject matter than in their style: Newman, Bradley, perhaps Maine and Bagehot. For interest in what one has to say, rather than conforming to or revolting from a conventional manner, is the essential thing."[12]

This remark may suggest that for Eliot the word *style* had become inherently pejorative. However, he distinguished

10. *Ibid.*, p. 155.
11. *To Criticize the Critic*, p. 39.
12. "Views and Reviews," *The New English Weekly* 7 (June 20, 1935): 190.

style that is an expression of the man from style in the good sense, which is an expression of the object. In 1927 Eliot wrote, of Richard of St. Victor,

> Sa prose me paraît répondre aux canons essentiels du style: il écrit ce qu'il pense dans les termes mêmes qui servent à le penser, sans enjolivement, métaphores ou figures, et en faisant abstraction de tout sentiment (car le sentiment, s'il est assez fort, se fera jour de toute façon; et, sinon, n'est pas à sa place). Elle pourrait servir de modèle de style aux écrivains anglais, au même titre, à mon avis, qu' Aristote, *The Drappier's* [*sic*] *Letters* de Swift, *The Principles of Logic* de F. H. Bradley et le premier volume des *Principia Mathematica* de Bertrand Russell.[13]

We examined in the last chapter Eliot's discussion of the dissociation of sensibility and his remarks on Tennyson and Browning as "reflective poets." In 1933 Eliot made much the same point about Arnold: "Just as his poetry is too reflective, too ruminative, to rise ever to the first rank, so also is his criticism."[14] At least once Eliot generalized this criticism, noting "the effort to construct a dream-world, which alters English poetry so greatly in the nineteenth century." Eliot called it "a problem of which various explanations may no doubt be found."[15] Probably the simplest and most comprehensive explanation is one well expressed by Swift, in "A Digression Concerning Madness": " 'Tis manifest what mighty advantages fiction has over truth; and the reason is just at our elbow, because imagination can build nobler scenes, and produce more wonderful revolutions than fortune or nature will be at expense to furnish." In Eliot's words, "Our lives are mostly a constant evasion of ourselves, and an evasion of the visible and sensible world."[16]

13. "Deux Attitudes Mystiques," *Le Roseau D'Or* 14 (1927): 157. It is to be noted that on p. 160 of this essay Eliot, or his translator, used the word *métaphore* for what we would call a *conceit*.

14. *The Use of Poetry*, p. 122.

15. "Andrew Marvell," *Selected Essays*, p. 259.

16. *The Use of Poetry*, p. 155.

Eliot's point is surely not that Englishmen were naturally more inclined to daydream in the nineteenth century than they had been in the eighteenth. The difference is rather in the degree of encouragement that the prevailing critical attitude gave to this natural tendency. What it meant to have a Coleridge instead of a Swift presiding at the beginning of a century can easily be imagined. In fact, Eliot traced back to one main source the influence that, until the nineteenth century, tended to discourage introspection. Contrasting the "day-dreamy feeling" of a poem by William Morris with the "bright, hard precision" of one by Marvell, Eliot observed, "Marvell is no greater personality than William Morris, but he had something much more solid behind him: he had the vast and penetrating influence of Ben Jonson."[17]

I have tried to give, not a comprehensive classification of all the species of self-consciousness with which Eliot deals, but a representative sample. We may now take a broad view of the subject. In Eliot's view, one of the most important tendencies in modern intellectual history is a progressive development of self-consciousness. In the last chapter we examined the development, starting at least as far back as Descartes, of the psychological point of view in philosophy. During the early part of Eliot's career, this process was culminating in the establishment of psychology as a discipline independent of philosophy; one of the major themes of Eliot's thesis, as we have seen, was a denial that there could be any such science as psychology, at least as it was conceived by many of its proponents. Eliot's critical aim, "to divert interest from the poet to the poetry" (that is, his opposition to all tendencies toward the psychological point of view in criticism, whether caused by Romantic aesthetics, psychoanalytic criticism, or even humanism), must be understood against this background.

Probably the most important cause of self-consciousness

17. "Andrew Marvell," *Selected Essays*, pp. 258–60.

as a characteristic of modern culture is the development of the historical sense. In an essay of 1929, which should certainly be reprinted, "Experiment in Criticism," Eliot wrote that "modern criticism begins with . . . Sainte-Beuve." He explained:

> Where he differed from previous French critics was in his implicit conception of literature, not only as a body of writings to be enjoyed, but as a process of change in history, and as a part of the study of history. The notion that literary values are relative to literary periods, that the literature of a period is primarily an expression and a symptom of the time, is so natural to us now that we can hardly detach our minds from it. We can hardly conceive that the degree and kind of self-consciousness which we have could ever not have been. How much criticism of contemporary literature is taken up with discussing whether, and in what degree, this book or novel or poem is expressive of our mentality, of the personality of our age; and how often our critics seemed to be interested rather in inquiring what we (including themselves) are like, than with the book, novel, or poem as a work of art!

He goes on to suggest that the critics of the seventeenth and eighteenth centuries "had really a great deal more faith in themselves than we have" and concludes by quoting the end of Sainte-Beuve's study of Port Royal: "He who had it most at heart to know his object, whose ambition was most engaged in seizing it, whose pride was most alert to paint it—how powerless he feels, and how far beneath his task, on the day when, seeing it almost finished and the result obtained, he feels his exaltation sink, feels himself overcome by faintness and inevitable disgust, and perceives in his turn that he too is only a fleeting illusion in the midst of the infinite illusory flux!"[18]

18. "Experiment in Criticism," *The Bookman* 70 (November 1929): 225, 228, and 229. Eliot made precisely the same point in a comparison of the Elizabethan and Jacobean dramatists with the nineteenth-century French novelists in *Selected Essays*, pp. 178–79.

The danger that Eliot saw in the historical sense is implied in his extenuation of Johnson's inability to appreciate the versification of Donne and of Milton's *Lycidas:* "What is lacking is an historical sense which was not yet due to appear. . . . If the eighteenth century had admired the poetry of earlier times in the way in which we can admire it, the result would have been chaos: there would have been no eighteenth century as we know it. That age would not have had the conviction necessary for perfecting the kinds of poetry that it did perfect."[19]

In Eliot's view, the problem of self-consciousness in the end comes down to a question of religion versus humanism; humanism is for Eliot the best of the alternatives to religion: "Man is man because he can recognize supernatural realities, not because he can invent them. Either everything in man can be traced as a development from below, or something must come from above. There is no avoiding that dilemma: you must be either a naturalist or a supernaturalist. If you remove from the word 'human' all that the belief in the supernatural has given to man, you can view him finally as no more than an extremely clever, adaptable, and mischievous little animal."[20] one of Eliot's fundamental objections to humanism is that it is a form of pragmatism. (Around the turn of the century, "Humanism" was used as a name for Pragmatism in its ethical aspect, as in the writings of F. C. S. Schiller.) "Humanism has much to say of Discipline and Order and Control; and I have parroted these terms myself," Eliot acknowledged. But he continued, "I found no discipline in humanism. . . . This I have found is only attainable through dogmatic religion. I do not say that dogmatic religion is justified because it supplies this need—*that is just the psychologism and the anthropocentrism that I wish to avoid*—but merely state my belief that in no

19. *On Poetry and Poets* (New York: Farrar, Straus and Giroux, 1961), p. 192.
20. "Second Thoughts about Humanism," *Selected Essays*, p. 433.

other way can the need be supplied."[21] Would the donkey continue to pursue the carrot if he were capable of seeing through the trick? As Eliot put it, "The great weakness of Pragmatism is that it ends by being of no *use* to anybody."[22]

Eliot indicated the implications for literary criticism of his objections to Humanism. As early as 1924, the reviewing of two works of anthropology suggested to Eliot a series of reflections: "The arts developed incidentally to the search for objects of talismanic properties. . . . At what point in civilisation does any conscious distinction between practical or magical utility and aesthetic beauty arise? . . . And a further question we should be impelled to ask is this: Is it possible and justifiable for art, the creation of beautiful objects and of literature, to persist indefinitely without its primitive purposes: is it possible for the aesthetic object to be a *direct* object of attention?"[23]

Humanism may be able, for a time, to maintain the value of the monuments of the past by reinterpreting them from a psychological point of view, by considering them, that is, as expressions of the minds of their authors rather than expressions of the objects (God, for example) attended to by those authors. But eventually it will become apparent that Humanism has trapped itself in Meno's dilemma—"A man cannot try to discover either what he knows or what he does not know." At that time, it will be

As, when an underground train, in the tube, stops too
    long between stations
And the conversation rises and slowly fades into
    silence

21. "Religion without Humanism," in *Humanism and America*, ed. Norman Foerster (New York: Farrar and Rinehart, 1930), p. 110. (Italics mine.)

22. "Francis Herbert Bradley," *Selected Essays*, pp. 403–4.

23. "[A review of] *The Growth of Civilisation* and *The Origin of Magic and Religion*," *The Criterion* 2 (July 1924): 490–91.

And you see behind every face the mental emptiness
    deepen
Leaving only the growing terror of nothing to think
    about.

(East Coker III)

This, I believe, is an accurate interpretation of Eliot's case against Humanism.

One of the reasons for Eliot's hostility to self-consciousness is that he believed it to lead to nihilism or pyrrhonism. Eliot's experience of life would simply appear to have set him apart from those who find the psychological point of view interesting and stimulating. One can find as early as his thesis the suggestion that the human mind, abstracted from its object, is devoid of interest: "The aim of my examination of structural psychology was to demonstrate that the more accurately and scientifically one pursues the traces of mentality in the 'mind' of the individual, the less one finds. . . . If you will find the mechanical anywhere, you will find it in the workings of mind; and to inspect living mind, you must look nowhere but in the world outside."[24] To the eye of hindsight the last clause appears pregnant with the principles of Eliot's early criticism.

Valéry was, for Eliot, the culmination, the perfection, so to speak, of the tendencies to self-consciousness characteristic of modern culture. He was the poet who most nearly effected "a complete severance between poetry and all beliefs" (the formula of I. A. Richards, the applicability of which to himself Eliot rejected). Two late essays on Valéry have a common theme: that "he was the most self-conscious of all poets" and that "his was . . . a profoundly destructive mind, even nihilistic," and that these two facts are intimately connected.[25]

<hr>

24. *Knowledge and Experience*, pp. 153–54.
25. "Leçon de Valéry," *The Listener* 37 (January 9, 1947): 72 and "From Poe to Valéry," in *To Criticize the Critic*, pp. 27–42.

To the extreme self-consciousness of Valéry must be added another trait: his extreme scepticism. It might be thought that such a man, without belief in anything which could be the subject of poetry, would find refuge in a doctrine of 'art for art's sake'. But Valéry was much too sceptical to believe even in art. It is significant, the number of times that he describes something he has written as an *ébauche*—a rough draft. He had ceased to believe in *ends*, and was only interested in *processes*. It often seems as if he had continued to write poetry, simply because he was interested in the introspective observation of himself engaged in writing it.[26]

In 1948 Eliot quoted a remark of Valéry's that states the quintessence of the psychological point of view: "In my opinion the most authentic philosophy is not in the objects of reflection, so much as in the very act of thought and its manipulation."[27] But we should take Eliot's remark about Valéry's nihilism not as personal moral censure or as an implication that Valéry was willfully destructive. He simply meant that Valéry carried further than any other poet, and with fewer illusions, the tendencies (many of them inevitable, according to Eliot) of the modern mind to self-consciousness: "It is he who will remain for posterity the representative poet, the symbol of the poet, of the first half of the twentieth century—not Yeats, not Rilke, not anyone else."[28]

There is another reason for Eliot's hostility to self-consciousness; it is an obstruction to, or even a substitute for, seeing the object. Consciousness of self and consciousness of object are linked together in Eliot's thought as mutually incompatible: "[Othello] has ceased to think about Desdemona, and is thinking about himself." In fact, when it becomes habitual, self-consciousness *is* solipsism: "To a man so occupied [as Byron] with himself and with the figure he was cutting nothing outside could be altogether real."[29] Solipsistic self-consciousness is one of the great

26. *To Criticize the Critic*, pp. 39–40.
27. *Ibid.*, p. 40.
28. "Leçon de Valéry," 72.
29. *On Poetry and Poets*, p. 226.

topics of Eliot's poetry as well as of his criticism, becoming explicit at least as early as the lines (412–17) on the key and the prison in *The Waste Land*. As Edward Chamberlayne puts it in *The Cocktail Party* (I. 3),

> What is hell? Hell is oneself,
> Hell is alone, the other figures in it
> Merely projections.

Perhaps these words are a literal statement of Eliot's theology.

We may turn to Eliot's thesis for a general theory of the problem of self-consciousness. In criticism of the psychologist's attempt to isolate for study the "contents of consciousness"—such as ideas, images, subjective feelings —which, according to the psychologist, stand between the subject and the object and through which subject knows object, Eliot asserted, "So far as they refer to their objects they are not themselves known, and *so far as they are made objects of knowledge they no longer refer to objects.*"[30]

The central idea of Eliot's theory of knowledge is that attention can at any given instant have only one direction; we can not at once know an object *and* be conscious of our knowing (though of course we may move from one of these acts to the other so quickly that, in practice, we believe that we *are* directly conscious of the object). Consequently, the fundamental act of knowledge, the moment when knower and known become one—that is, when our attention is concentrated *without distraction* upon the object—is something we can never be directly conscious of, "a fringe of indefinite extent, of feeling which we can only detect, so to speak, out of the corner of the eye and can never completely focus."[31] These moments of complete attention upon the object thus appear to be mere gaps, blanks, in our conscious, reflective life, though in fact they are the source of everything in that conscious life. This, I think, is one of

---

30. *Knowledge and Experience*, p. 62. (Emphasis mine.)
31. *On Poetry and Poets*, p. 93.

Eliot's most important ideas. Both his criticism and his poetry bear the mark of his continued meditation upon it. For him it is not a mere philosophical doctrine. It is precisely when approaching an idea like this one that Bradley was accustomed to advise the reader that if he wished to understand, his only course was to observe and to experiment for himself.

Eliot did not mean that conscious reflection upon, say, our image of a person gives no knowledge whatever. In fact, since the notion of knowledge without consciousness is meaningless, he is forced to admit that *only* through reflection can we have knowledge at all. But he insists on an important qualification—and here we may recall the words of Sir Henry Harcourt-Reilly in *The Cocktail Party* (I. 3),

> What we know of other people
> Is only our memory of the moments
> During which we knew them. And they have changed
> since then.

We think most easily of Eliot's insistence on the importance of permanence; we must not forget his insistence on the inevitability, and thus the importance, of change.

"Human kind cannot bear very much reality." The unified sensibility, the "condition of complete simplicity," is an ideal limit to be aimed at rather than a goal that is humanly attainable. It is only the saint who can approximate a condition of complete attention to his object, and that only after "a lifetime's death in love, / Ardour and selflessness and self-surrender."

> For most of us, there is only the unattended
> Moment, the moment in and out of time,
> The distraction fit, lost in a shaft of sunlight,
> The wild thyme unseen, or the winter lightning

Or the waterfall, or music heard so deeply
That it is not heard at all, but you are the music
While the music lasts.

(The Dry Salvages V)

The phrase "the distraction fit" can be glossed with a phrase from *Burnt Norton:* "distracted from distraction."

The doctrine expounded in Eliot's thesis, that there is no independent "real" world outside of our experiences but simply a multitude of interacting points of view, may appear, paradoxically, solipsistic. And there are indications that Eliot was not satisfied with Bradley's doctrine: "It is as difficult for Bradley as for Leibniz to maintain that there is any world at all, to find any objects for these mirrors to mirror."[32] Still, that doctrine did obviate the tendency toward self-consciousness implicit in the representational theory of knowledge. Bradley's neorealist opponents could not do as much, in Eliot's view; they were, in effect, simply returning to the position of Kant: "The thing is known through its appearances, but as soon as the distinction is made appearance and thing fall apart, and *appearance replaces thing as a point of attention.*"[33]

"To see the object as in itself it really is"—Arnold's phrase provided Eliot with a statement of the great central theme of his criticism, the theme that from beginning to end unifies and concentrates his critical thought, in its general, theoretical aspect. I do not claim that it is the explicit theme of all, or even of the majority, of Eliot's essays in practical criticism, his appreciations of individual writers. In these, his concern is not to argue the necessity of "looking steadily at the object" but to *practice* it himself. To put theory before practice in this instance would be precisely

32. *Knowledge and Experience,* p. 202.
33. *Ibid.,* p. 96. (Emphasis mine.)

to violate the spirit of that theory, which ought to be, if only it were possible, a "silent motto."

In the early criticism, Aristotle was Eliot's favorite example of a mind devoted to looking at the object. In "The Perfect Critic" he contrasted Aristotle with "the sentimental person, in whom a work of art arouses all sorts of emotions which have nothing to do with that work of art whatever, but are accidents of personal association," with the critic who likes "one poet because he reminds him of himself, or another because he expresses emotions which he admires," with the "dogmatic critic, who lays down a rule, who affirms a value," with Coleridge, who is "apt to take leave of the data of criticism, and arouse the suspicion that he has been diverted into a metaphysical hare-and-hounds," with Hegel, who dealt "with his emotions as if they were definite objects which had aroused those emotions."[34] But Aristotle, he claimed, "had none of these impure desires to satisfy; in whatever sphere of interest, he looked solely and steadfastly at the object."[35]

It is this theme that clearly distinguishes Eliot's criticism from the tradition of Romantic criticism, to which it is quite similar in other respects. Perhaps the majority of modern schools of criticism appear, from Eliot's perspective, to encourage the psychological point of view: historical criticism, biographical criticism, psychoanalytic criticism, Humanism, the critical positions of Arnold and of I. A. Richards (the last three of these can be classed together as promoting "religion without an object"). Almost the whole force of Eliot's critical thought is applied to directing the attention outward, onto the object. In the case of a thinker who is not a naïve realist, looking at the object can best be defined as escape from preoccupation with self, from reflection, from self-dramatization. In "The Perfect Critic,"

34. *The Sacred Wood*, 2nd ed. (London: Methuen, 1960), pp. 7, 11, 13, and 9.
35. *Ibid.*, p. 11.

Eliot described the goal he aimed at: "The end of the enjoyment of poetry is a pure contemplation from which all the accidents of personal emotion are removed; thus we aim to see the object as it really is and find a meaning for the words of Arnold."[36]

Eliot's great theme can often be found embodied in concrete critical judgments. One of the most interesting instances is a comparison of Machiavelli and Hobbes. Eliot begins with the paradox that because "Machiavelli is wholly *devoted*—to his task of his own place and time . . . he arrives at a far greater impersonality and detachment than Hobbes." The explanation is that "Hobbes is not passionately moved by the spectacle of national disaster: he is interested in his own theory." In other words, Hobbes's detachment, as against Machiavelli's, is *indifference.* Observe the next step in the argument, the result of Hobbes's self-consciousness: "[Hobbes] is interested in his own theory; and we can see his theory as partly an outcome of the weaknesses and distortions of his own temperament. . . . For true cynicism is a fault of the temperament of the observer, not a conclusion arising naturally out of the contemplation of the obect; it is quite the reverse of 'facing facts.' " Eliot is now ready to fix his own definition of "impersonality" (awareness of which would obviate many of the objections that have been made against his "Impersonal theory of poetry"): "In Machiavelli there is no cynicism whatever. No trace of the weaknesses and failures of his own life and character mars the clear glass of his vision. In detail, no doubt, where the meanings of words suffer a slight alteration, we feel a conscious irony; but his total view was unimpaired by any such emotional colour. Such a view of life as Machiavelli's implies a state of the soul which may be called a state of innocence. A view like Hobbes's is slightly theatrical and almost sentimental." And he concludes that Ma-

36. *Ibid.*, pp. 14–15.

chiavelli "provides one more piece of evidence that great intellectual power arises from great passions."[37] Eliot has accomplished nothing less than a revaluation—almost a transvaluation—of the word "impersonality," and the new meaning is consistent with, and convincingly supported by, his whole critical thought.

In "From Poe to Valéry," Eliot predicted that the "fearful progress in self-consciousness" in modern poetry was near its end. "I believe that the *art poétique* of which we find the germ in Poe, and which bore fruit in the work of Valéry, has gone as far as it can go. I do not believe that this aesthetic can be of any help to later poets." But then he added, "What will take its place I do not know. An aesthetic which merely contradicted it would not do. To insist on the all-importance of subject-matter, to insist that the poet should be spontaneous and irreflective, that he should depend upon inspiration and neglect technique, would be a lapse from what is in any case a highly civilized attitude to a barbarous one."[38] As these words suggest, I have so far presented only one side of Eliot's attitude to self-consciousness.

In his thesis Eliot took a position at the exact mid-point between behaviorism and subjective idealism. So far we have been considering the dangers of the latter of these extremes. But there would also be a danger of moving too far toward behaviorism. If totally without self-consciousness, man would be "that which is only moved / And has in it no source of movement—" moving "In appetency, on its metalled ways / Of time past and time future."[39]

Eliot saw the development of the civilized mind out of the primitive mind as a movement from pure behavior toward solipsistic self-consciousness. To rebuke a historian of the

37. "Nicolo Machiavelli," *The Times Literary Supplement*, June 16, 1927, [p. 413].
38. *To Criticize the Critic*, p. 41.
39. *The Dry Salvages* V and *Burnt Norton* III.

sacred dance for "formulating intelligible reasons for the primitive dancer's dancing," Eliot invented a parable:

> It is equally possible to assert that primitive man acted in a certain way and then found a reason for it. An unoccupied person, finding a drum, may be seized with a desire to beat it; but unless he is an imbecile he will be unable to continue beating it, and thereby satisfying a need (rather than a "desire"), without finding a reason for so doing. The reason may be the long continued drought. The next generation or the next civilization will find a more plausible reason for beating a drum. Shakespeare and Racine—or rather the developments which led up to them—each found his own reason. The reasons may be divided into tragedy and comedy. We still have similar reasons, but we have lost the drum.[40]

Shakespeare and Racine are, no doubt, at the ideal midpoint between behavior and solipsism, the point at which reflection is *recognition,* when it functions as a "development of sensibility" and not as a substitute for it. The passage above may be compared with two quoted earlier in this chapter—the one in which Eliot suggested that "it is perhaps epistemology . . . that has given us the fine arts" and the one about the historical development of poetry from emphasis on subject matter to emphasis on style.

Self-consciousness can be useful, provided its function is critical rather than creative (without overlooking "the capital importance of criticism in the work of creation itself"[41]). In his several essays on Humanism, Eliot's purpose was not to deny its great value but to place it in proper relation to religion: "To exist at all, [Humanism] is dependent upon some other attitude, for it is essentially critical—I would even say parasitical. . . . Both Socrates and Erasmus were content to remain critics, and to leave the religious fabric

40. "The Beating of a Drum," *The Nation & The Athenaeum* 34 (October 6, 1923): 12.
41. "The Function of Criticism," *Selected Essays,* p. 18.

untouched."[42] For Eliot, creation is properly passive, in the sense that it is not controlled by the conscious will but by the object; the proper function of the conscious will is critical. "The bad poet," he pointed out, "is usually unconscious where he ought to be conscious, and conscious where he ought to be unconscious."[43]

But the ultimate justification of reflection is not that it is useful: "It would appear that criticism, like any philosophical activity, is inevitable and requires no justification."[44] Similarly, of the historical sense that separates us from Samuel Johnson, Eliot wrote, "If we have arrived at this historical sense ourselves, our only course is to develop it further." But then it turns out that the way forward is also the way backward: "One of the ways in which we can develop it in ourselves is through an understanding of a critic in whom it is not apparent."[45]

In the "Introduction" to *The Use of Poetry and the Use of Criticism,* Eliot defended criticism against those who call it "an occupation of decadence, and a symptom, if not a cause, of the creative impotence of a people." Of "the change from a pre-critical to a critical age," Eliot insisted that it is "inseparable from social changes on a vast scale, such changes as have always taken place and always will." He concluded this defense of criticism with an interesting remark, that will bring us to the topic of the next chapter: "The important moment for the appearance of criticism seems to be the time when poetry ceases to be the expression of the mind of a whole people."[46]

42. "The Humanism of Irving Babbitt," *Selected Essays,* pp. 421 and 422.
43. "Tradition and the Individual Talent," *Selected Essays,* p. 10.
44. *The Use of Poetry,* p. 19.
45. *On Poetry and Poets,* p. 192.
46. Pp. 20–22.

5
Personality: The Individual versus the Social Points of View

The Sacred Wood as a whole is often taken to embody the "Impersonal theory of poetry" announced in "Tradition and the Individual Talent." But a close examination of the book shows that the word "impersonal" is sometimes used with unfavorable connotations. For example, Blake is praised for escaping "the ordinary processes of society which constitute education for the ordinary man. For these processes consist largely in the acquisition of impersonal ideas which obscure what we really are and feel, what we really want, and what really excites our interest."[1] And the defect of Massinger's work is found to be "precisely a defect of personality. He is not, however, the only man of letters who, at the moment when a new view of life is wanted, has looked at life through the eyes of his predecessors."[2]

It is not difficult to find the point of view that makes consistent the apparent contradictions in Eliot's use of the word "impersonal." This point of view could be called tentatively "stoicism." Of course Eliot never called himself

1. "Blake," *The Sacred Wood,* 2nd ed. (London: Methuen, 1960), p. 154, and *Selected Essays,* 2nd ed. (New York: Harcourt, Brace and World, 1960), p. 277.
2. "Philip Massinger," *The Sacred Wood,* p. 143, and *Selected Essays,* p. 195.

113

a stoic, and he was probably never influenced by the stoic philosophers. I mean only that in *The Sacred Wood* it is implied that there is a false impersonality which results from the uncritical acceptance of the values and opinions of society and that a strong personality is necessary to "slough off" this false impersonality and to achieve a true impersonality: submission of the individual will to the laws of the universe.[3] A real influence would be the philosophy (and perhaps the life) of Spinoza: "When we understand necessity, as Spinoza knew, we are free because we assent."[4] A precise statement of Eliot's early attitude to personality is the epigraph to "The Perfect Critic," from Gourmont: "Eriger en lois ses impressions personnelles, c'est le grand effort d'un homme s'il est sincère."

The fact is that Eliot's high valuation of personality in one sense and his rejection of it in another are not only not contradictory but are complementary. The doctrine of points of view set forth in Eliot's thesis anticipates and in part serves to explain his subsequent efforts to define the claims of the individual as against society and also reveals the connection of this problem with that of personality. A sentence from the "Conclusion" of the thesis well formulates the intransigence of the conflict between the individual and society: "We may put ourselves at the individual or the social point of view, as we please; but we must not forget that unless we make allowance at the start for the equality of their claims to validity we shall be left with a most uncomfortable hiatus, for we can never deduce the one from the other."[5] Earlier passages of the thesis explain

3. "La vie est un dépouillement. Le but de l'activité propre de l'homme est de nettoyer sa personnalité, de la laver de toutes les souillures qu'y déposa l'éducation, de la dégager de toutes les empreintes qu'y laissèrent nos admirations adolescentes." Remy de Gourmont, quoted in "Philip Massinger," *The Sacred Wood*, p. 139, and *Selected Essays*, pp. 192–93.

4. "The Perfect Critic," *The Sacred Wood*, p. 11.

5. *Knowledge and Experience* (New York: Farrar, Straus and Company, 1964), p. 159.

precisely what Eliot meant by this statement. "We intend, from our divers limited points of view, a single real world, and we forget that metaphysically this real world is only real so far as it finds realization through these points of view. . . . I repeat then that the objective world is only actual in one or other point of view, but that each point of view intends to be, not a point of view, but the world one and impersonal."[6] To these sentences I will add one more, and the situation is complete: "It is only so long as we can support a particular point of view (and this involves not recognizing it as such) that we can believe that the contradiction between truth and error is superseded."[7] (I should explain that the "social point of view" as Eliot uses the term here has no specific content; it is not related to any specific society. It is any situation that forces the individual to regard his own point of view from the "outside," perceiving that it is not "the world one and impersonal" but in fact only one of many possible points of view.) I ask the reader to study these sentences carefully and to refer to them if necessary in the following pages as I attempt to explicate them.

We may note first the origin of "personality" in the bad sense. According to Eliot's theory it should develop when the individual accepts his point of view as nothing more than a point of view (rather than "the world one and impersonal"), not being able to sustain that point of view vis-à-vis the other points if view of which he is conscious. His attention is reflected inwards upon the contents of his own mind rather than upon the object. He becomes aware of his "ideas" or "feelings" as distinct from objects, when he becomes aware that the objects are regarded differently from other points of view. We found in chapter 3 that this very same process is the cause of the dissociation of sensi-

6. *Ibid.*, p. 90.
7. *Ibid.*, p. 121.

bility. As Eliot expressed it in the terminology of his thesis, "It is only in social behaviour, in the conflict and readjustment of finite centres, that feelings and things are torn apart."[8] The self may come to seem more real than the "external" world. It is this sense of "personality" as a self-conscious point of view that Eliot attacks in the early criticism. As a general theory of the origin of personality, this explanation may or may not convince (it seems to me of considerable interest as such), but that problem need not disturb us here. What is immediately relevant is that Eliot's formula for the unacceptable kind of personality does correspond to the theory held and perhaps practiced by subjective idealists: "the world is my representation." It is precisely against such a view as Pater's that Eliot directed his destructive analysis of personality. Such a view becomes the nightmare vision of solipsism that evokes horror in Eliot's poetry, early and late: "the final desolation / Of solitude in the phantasmal world / Of imagination, shuffling memories and desires" (*The Cocktail Party*).

It can now be seen that one way to avoid becoming a "personality" in this bad sense is to assert the individual point of view against the social. It is this position, set forth in the early criticism, that I have tentatively labeled as "stoicism." Before proceeding, however, we should recall that the concept of the individual point of view on which the early criticism is based does not allow for unrestrained individualism. If one's reaction to the conflict of the individual with the social point of view is not pyrrhonism but scepticism (Eliot often pointedly distinguished the two), one's effort is to sustain the personal point of view.[9] This

8. *Ibid.*, pp. 24–25.
9. "Scepticism is a highly civilised trait, though, when it declines into pyrrhonism, it is one of which civilisation can die. Where scepticism is strength, pyrrhonism is weakness: for we need not only the strength to defer a decision, but the strength to make one." *Notes towards the Definition of Culture*, in *Christianity and Culture* (New York: Harcourt, Brace and Company, 1949), p. 102.

self-assertion is *critical* rather than naïve and is, in fact, not an assertion of self but of one's "world." The individual point of view is to be constructed of "objective correlatives" and its form—logic, in the sense of consistency—is also universal rather than personal.

But once this qualification is made, we can say that, whatever "Tradition and the Individual Talent" may suggest to the contrary, Eliot's early criticism affirms, even to an unusual degree, the value of "personality" in the sense of a unique point of view. This is best brought out in an essay that appeared in the issue of *The Egoist* previous to the one containing "Tradition and the Individual Talent" and that gives a much warmer, more intimate expression to the living writer's sense of his relation to his predecessors: "This relation is a feeling of profound kinship, or rather of a peculiar personal intimacy, with another, probably a dead author. It may overcome us suddenly, on first or after long acquaintance; it is certainly a crisis; and when a young writer is seized with his first passion of this sort he may be changed, metamorphosed almost, within a few weeks even, from a bundle of second-hand sentiments into a person. The imperative intimacy arouses for the first time a real, an unshakeable confidence."[10] One may surmise that the somewhat frigid tone of the famous essay that followed was due to a need to compensate for the uncharacteristic warmth expressed in this earlier essay. And the *tone* of "Tradition and the Individual Talent" has done something, I think, to mislead interpretation of its *ideas* and, in fact, of Eliot's early criticism.

Eliot's early criticism affirms the value of personality, in one sense of that treacherous word, to a degree not less but greater than does almost any earlier English criticism, with the exception of Pater and his school. We must bear in mind, however, that the aim of asserting one's personality

10. "Reflections on Contemporary Poetry," *The Egoist* 4 (July 1919): 39.

in the good sense is, according to Eliot's early position, the *alternative* to becoming a personality in the bad sense. The two kinds of personality are distinguished by a very fine line. The essential distinction is in the direction of attention: "No artist produces great art by a deliberate attempt to express his personality. He expresses his personality indirectly through concentrating upon a task which is a task in the same sense as the making of an efficient engine or the turning of a jug or a table-leg."[11] It is just here, in trying to define this precarious distinction between personality in the good and in the bad sense, that we can appreciate the importance of *belief* for Eliot. The following passage, from late in Eliot's career, is a statement of precisely the same dilemma formulated in the sentences from his thesis that I have taken for my text. In 1947, Eliot was concerned to define, in retrospect, the *"Leçon de Valéry"*:

> Valéry has been called a philosopher. But a philosopher, in the ordinary sense, is a man who constructs or supports a philosophic system; and in this sense, we can say that Valéry was too intelligent to be a philosopher. The constructive philosopher must have a religious faith, or some substitute for a religious faith; and generally he is only able to construct because of his ability to blind himself to other points of view, or to remain unconscious of the emotive causes which attach him to his particular system. Valéry was much too conscious to be able to philosophise in this way; and so his 'philosophy' lays itself open to the accusation of being only an elaborate game. Precisely, but to be able to play this game, to be able to take delight in it, is one of the manifestations of civilised man. There is only one higher stage possible for civilised men: that is to unite the profoundest scepticism with the deepest faith. But Valéry was not Pascal. . . . [Valéry's] was, I think, a profoundly destructive mind, even nihilistic.[12]

This passage is one of a long series of attempts to solve the crucial problem of the function of belief in the composi-

11. "Four Elizabethan Dramatists," *Selected Essays*, p. 96.
12. "Leçon de Valéry," *The Listener* 37 (January 9, 1947): 72.

tion and in the enjoyment of poetry, to find a middle position between "pure poetry" on the one hand and "propaganda" on the other. Some of the most important discussions are in the note to section II of the essay "Dante," in
"Arnold and Pater," in "Propaganda and Poetry," and in
the essays on Humanism, but in fact seldom is Eliot's criticism far away from this theme. I shall explore further, in
chapter 6, "Form," implications for literary criticism of the
problem of belief.

But now we must return to the conflict between the individual point of view (from which we believe that our world
is "the world one and impersonal") and the social point of
view (from which we recognize that our world is only one
of many points of view). For the "stoicism" of the early
criticism did not prove to be a definitive solution to this
conflict. In fact, I called Eliot's early attitude "stoic" because of his radical *reaction* against stoicism in the two essays on Seneca written in 1927 (note the date). He wrote,
in "Shakespeare and the Stoicism of Seneca," "A man does
not join himself with the Universe so long as he has anything else to join himself with; men who could take part in
the life of a thriving Greek city-state had something better
to join themselves to; and Christians have had something
better. Stoicism is the refuge for the individual in an indifferent or hostile world too big for him."[13] This is a comment on a passage by Chapman, which had earlier been one
of Eliot's favorite touchstones: "A man to join himself with
the Universe."

We have observed that the distinction between the two
kinds of personality recognized in Eliot's early criticism is
a fine one. And, if one comes to accept the social point of
view as of greater validity than the individual—if one *takes*
the social point of view—then that distinction virtually
disappears. As Eliot expressed it in comparing Roman (and
Elizabethan) Stoicism with modern subjective idealism

13. *Selected Essays*, p. 112.

(Nietzsche), "There is not much difference between identifying oneself with the Universe and identifying the Universe with oneself."[14]

But only confusion could follow from the attempt to see this change of attitude as absolute, in relation to the earlier criticism, or, I might add, as definitive, in relation to the later. Before going on, I take this opportunity to say something in a general way about the kind of consistency to be found in the development of Eliot's critical view. The fact is that almost all of the diverse, and sometimes conflicting, values invoked in Eliot's criticism are present from the beginning; there are passages describing the value of a social background in literature even in the period of *The Sacred Wood*. The first and second parts of the essay on Blake, for example, deliberately weigh against each other the advantages and the disadvantages of the assertion of the self against the cultural background. Eliot's description of the development of attitude in Donne is a very apt description of his own development: "One of the characteristics of Donne which wins him, I fancy, his interest for the present age, is his fidelity to emotion as he finds it; his recognition of the complexity of feeling and its rapid alterations and antitheses. A change of feeling, with Donne, is rather the regrouping of the same elements under a mood which was previously subordinate: it is not the substitution of one mood for a wholly different one. . . . The mind has unity and order."[15] (We may make this passage do double duty; note that it is a good statement in practical terms of the concept of the point of view and of the way one point of view develops into another one.) There are, if you wish, "inconsistencies" in Eliot's critical view, but the practice of citing instances as if they demonstrated the fundamental

14. *Ibid.*, pp. 119–20.
15. "John Donne," *The Nation & The Athenaeum* 33 (June 9, 1923): 332.

bankruptcy of that view is a very imperfect substitute for trying to understand.

On the other hand, once this qualification has been made, one must not underestimate the significance of what we might now call changes of emphasis in Eliot's criticism. That criticism is just not to be understood without taking into account its chronological development. The following quotations will give a general impression of that development. In May 1922 Eliot wrote, "But a truly independent way of looking at things, a point of view which cannot be sorted under any known religious or political title; in fact, the having the only thing which gives a work pretending to literary art its justification; the having something which the public have not got: this is always detested."[16] But in September 1927 he wrote, "[Blake] made a Universe; and very few people can do that. But the fact that the gift is rare does not make it necessarily valuable. It is not any one man's business to make a Universe; and what any one man can make in this way is not, in the end, so good or so useful as the ordinary Universe which we all make together."[17] Here we seem to have an absolute change and even a public repudiation of the concept of the individual point of view on which the early criticism is based. But of course this is not the expression of the whole of Eliot's mind. Three years later he wrote the almost romantic description of Baudelaire as walking "secure in this high vocation, that he was capable of a damnation denied to the politicians and the newspaper editors of Paris."[18] And in 1936 we have, in the essay "In Memoriam," the disconcertingly radical criticism of Tennyson's compromise with his society. These essays on Baudelaire and Tennyson suggest to me that we are not

16. "London Letter," *The Dial* 72 (May 1922): 511.
17. "The Mysticism of Blake," *The Nation & The Athenaeum* 41 (September 17, 1927): 779.
18. "Baudelaire," *Selected Essays*, p. 380.

meant to smile at Harry Monchensey when he remarks of
his injured brother:

> A minor trouble like a concussion
> Cannot make very much difference to John.
> A brief vacation from the kind of consciousness
> That John enjoys, can't make very much difference
> To him or to anyone else.

When, eleven years after writing *The Family Reunion,* Eliot
revealed that "my hero now strikes me as an insufferable
prig," he was, I think, expressing, not his original intention,
but his subsequent recognition.[19]

(It is interesting to regard Eliot's own play about "the
guilt of a mother" in the light of the essay of twenty years
earlier, "Hamlet and his Problems." Harry's petty and realistic complaints about his mother, which begin Act II, fail
to provide the objective correlative for his mystical agony
of Act I to a degree that makes Shakespeare's play seem
luminous in comparison.)

The last paragraph but one shows the reason for the
persistence, after 1927, of the "egoistic" attitude in Eliot:
it is connected for him with the genesis of the religious
attitude. One of the explanations, in Eliot's thought, of the
religious consciousness is that it arises when we contem-
plate "what we really are and feel, what we really want, and
what really excites our interest," find the present reality
insufficient to the vision, and thus turn to an ideal world in
which they will be realized. In 1919 he wrote, in a review
of an edition of Donne's sermons, that the sermon of the
age, and in fact Elizabethan-Jacobean prose in general,
does not possess "the permanent qualities of the true work
of art" because it does not allow for "direct personal com-

19. "Poetry and Drama," *On Poetry and Poets* (New York: Farrar, Straus and
Giroux, 1961), p. 91.

munication." We find "but very seldom, in the prose of Donne's age, but seldom, as in this passage, the sense of the artist as an Eye curiously, patiently watching himself as a man. 'There is the Ego, the particular, the individuall, I.' Donne was an Egoist, but not an egoist of the religious, the mystical type. . . . 'Amourous soule, ambitious soule, covetous soule, voluptuous soule, what wouldest thou have in heaven?' We should like to know that, but Donne cannot tell us. . . . He is no Buddha."[20]

On the other hand, the social point of view can support religious values. This can be seen in Eliot's rejection of the Humanism of Babbitt. Eliot's premise was that there had been no self-sustaining tradition of humanism. From this he concluded, "Our problem being to form the future, we can only form it on the materials of the past; we must *use* our heredity, instead of denying it."[21] For a defense of religion *against* humanism, this argument is remarkably humanistic in tendency; and of course we notice that here Eliot was using that favorite device of turning an opponent's arguments against him. But even when we have allowed for this, we find that this attitude is well represented in Eliot elsewhere. I think it began to develop in the early twenties and reached fulfillment in the mellow catholicism of taste (or at least, of sympathy) of the last essays. It seems to me to be a point of view almost sharply distinguishable from that of the essays on Baudelaire or Tennyson.

In fact, I think that the course of Eliot's career as a dramatist reveals the process and the result of a struggle between the (egoistically) religious and the (religiously) social points of view. In *The Family Reunion* very little sympathy, to say the least, seems to be shown to the ordinary

20. "The Preacher as Artist," *The Athenaeum* (November 28, 1919), pp. 1252–53.
21. "The Humanism of Irving Babbitt," *Selected Essays*, p. 421.

social consciousness, when it conflicts with the incipient religious vocation of Harry. In *The Cocktail Party* two "ways" are presented sympathetically. And in the last plays there is hardly any overt distinction at all between the religious and the humanistic points of view. Perhaps these plays *consciously* realize Eliot's own program: "What I want is a literature which should be *un*consciously, rather than deliberately and defiantly, Christian."[22]

There is, however, another reason for the persistence of individualism in Eliot. In his thesis Eliot argued that the ultimate *matter* of reality—or, if you like, the closest possible approach to reality—was the immediate experience of the individual. If you *deny* the validity of individual experience in the name of the social point of view, you are left with nothing but unreal abstractions; there is no immediate social experience. Eliot's sense that immediate personal experience, however much it is or ought to be transcended, is the indispensable material of reality persists throughout his career. In 1935 he wrote, "Direct knowledge of life is knowledge directly in relation to ourselves. . . . Knowledge of life obtained through fiction . . . can only be a knowledge of other people's knowledge of life, not of life itself."[23]

It is at this point that we may appropriately attempt to define the relation of Eliot's sociological writings to his critical view. The key to understanding Eliot's sociological thought, I believe, is to realize that it is inseparable from, that in fact it arises from, his concern with individual psychology. This has been more than suggested by the discussion so far; what remains is to tie the threads together more securely.

The most convenient place to start is with the two remarkable essays on Seneca written in 1927. In these, Eliot is concerned to analyze the causes of "Elizabethan in-

22. "Religion and Literature," *Selected Essays*, p. 346.
23. *Ibid.*, p. 349.

dividualism" and to suggest its continuity with Roman Stoicism in one direction and with modern individualism
("Nietzsche . . . is a late variant") in another: "What influence the work of Seneca and Machiavelli and Montaigne
seems to me to exert in common on that time, and most
conspicuously through Shakespeare, is an influence toward
a kind of self-consciousness that is new; the self-consciousness and self-dramatization of the Shakespearean hero, of
whom Hamlet is only one."[24] Of course, Eliot does not
suggest that the influence of Seneca operated in a vacuum;
the appeal of Seneca was that Elizabethan England, like
Imperial Rome, was "a period of dissolution and chaos;
and in such a period any emotional attitude which seems to
give a man something firm, even if it be only the attitude
of 'I am myself alone,' is eagerly taken up."[25]

A suggestive sentence devoted to an analysis of the rise
of Roman Stoicism contains the germ of the sociological
thought that Eliot was later to elaborate: "Whether the
Roman scepticism was, as Nisard suggests, the result of a
too rapid and great expansion and mixture of races cancell-
ing each other's beliefs, rather than the product of a lively
inquiring intelligence, the 'beliefs' of Stoicism are a consequence of scepticism; and the ethic of Seneca's plays is that
of an age which supplied the lack of moral habits by a
system of moral attitudes and poses."[26] In chapter 3 we
found that the dissociation of sensibility was the result of
reflection, of self-consciousness, of directing the attention
inwards upon the "contents" of the mind. In the present
chapter we have found that the origin of personality in the
bad sense is the very same process; it is "self-dramatization," "a system of moral attitudes and poses." And these
passages just quoted clearly indicate the cause of self-con-

24. "Shakespeare and the Stoicism of Seneca," *Selected Essays,* p. 119.
25. *Ibid.,* p. 112.
26. "Seneca in Elizabethan Translation," *Selected Essays,* p. 58.

sciousness in scepticism, and the cause of scepticism in turn in the dissolution of a unified and "organic" social perspective into irreconcilable points of view. (In 1947 Eliot, though declining to seek for the ultimate causes of the dissociation of sensibility, asserted that in England "it had something to do with the Civil War."[27]) In fact, the sentence with which I began this paragraph is the last step in an argument in which Eliot attempted to explain why the plays of Seneca, in comparison with those of the Greek dramatists, exhibit "a development of language exceeding the development of sensibility."[28] This formula is almost exactly the same one Eliot had used seven years earlier in analyzing the dissociation of sensibility in Massinger.[29] The problems of individual psychology—the dissociation of sensibility and the development of self-conscious personality—cannot be isolated from the problems of society.

But the problem is even more complicated. The last passage on Roman Stoicism also indicates that the whole problem is ultimately one of religious *belief.* However, the phrase *moral habits* in that passage suggests a qualification at this point. Eliot often makes a very interesting distinction, suggesting that in a healthy society what is required, at least of the majority of men, is not so much belief as "acceptance."[30] *Belief,* I suppose, is too self-conscious to be tolerable to all but a few. And, as Eliot remarked years later, "Even for the most highly developed and conscious individual, living in the world, a consciously Christian direction of thought and feeling can only occur at particular mo-

27. "Milton II," *On Poetry and Poets,* p. 173.
28. "Seneca in Elizabethan Translation," *Selected Essays,* p. 57. For the whole discussion see pp. 53–57.
29. "Massinger's feeling for language had outstripped his feeling for things." *The Sacred Wood,* p. 128, and *Selected Essays,* p. 185.
30. "But poetry can be penetrated by a philosophic idea, it can deal with this idea when it has reached the point of immediate acceptance, when it has become almost a physical modification." "Dante," *The Sacred Wood,* pp. 162–63. See also p. 237 of the other essay on Dante, in *Selected Essays.*

ments during the day and during the week, and these moments themselves recur in consequence of formed habits;
to be conscious, without remission, of a Christian and a
non-Christian alternative at moments of choice, imposes a
very great strain."[31] A clear-cut opposition between belief
and habit would be a form of dissociation of sensibility. In
short, we have encountered the same insoluble knot of
mutual implications among the personal, the social, and
the religious that we found in the old problem of Enthusiasm and Superstition in chapter 1. In fact, it is the thesis of
Notes towards the Definition of Culture that this knot *is* insoluble: "We may go further and ask whether what we call the
culture, and what we call the religion, of a people are not
different aspects of the same thing; the culture being, essentially, the incarnation (so to speak) of the religion of a
people."[32]

When we perceive the starting point of Eliot's sociology
in his concern for the unified sensibility of the individual,
we can understand why, for him, the ideal society must be
a class society—more specifically, a society based on an
ordered hierarchy of values, as in the Platonic model. But
it should be observed that Eliot's attitude is not here merely
negative; the purpose of a class system is not solely to
prevent too great conflict between different points of view
or even solely to facilitate the growth of communal solidarity by breaking down the society as a whole into groups with
common interests. Eliot always stresses the necessity for

31. *The Idea of a Christian Society,* in *Christianity and Culture,* p. 24. Compare
Aristotle: "Now some think that we are made good by nature, others by habitua-
tion, others by teaching. Nature's part evidently does not depend on us, but as
a result of some divine causes is present in those who are truly fortunate; while
argument and teaching, we may suspect, are not powerful with all men, but the
soul of the student must first have been cultivated by means of habits for noble
joy and noble hatred, like earth which is to nourish the seed." *Nicomachean Ethics*
1179b20–26, *The Works of Aristotle,* ed. W.D. Ross, 12 vols. (Oxford: Oxford
University Press, 1908–52), 9: n. pag.
32. P. 101.

diversity within unity rather than uniformity. I shall pursue this subject further in chapter 6, Form, examining several interesting passages in which Eliot expresses his sense of the advantages of a dramatist's addressing an audience, like Shakespeare's, of various levels of education and sensitivity.

Approaching Eliot's sociology as we have, we can also see why he should be driven to hint, as he does several times, something so daring as that the effort must be made to convert the world to Christianity.[33] And in 1930 he wrote,

> I believe that at the present time the problem of the unification of the world and the problem of the unification of the individual, are in the end one and the same problem; and that the solution of one is the solution of the other. Analytical psychology (even if accepted far more enthusiastically than I can accept it) can do little except produce monsters; for it is attempting to produce unified individuals in a world without unity; the social, political, and economic sciences can do little, for they are attempting to produce the great society with an aggregation of human beings who are not units but merely bundles of incoherent impulses and beliefs. The problem of nationalism and the problem of dissociated personalities may turn out to be the same.[34]

This would seem to be the *ne plus ultra* of the extension outwards of the implications of individual psychology.

We have seen that for Eliot the conflict of the individual and the social points of view is, *in the abstract,* intransigent. The aim of his sociological writings is to define the idea of

33. "Without a common faith, all efforts towards drawing nations closer together in culture can produce only an illusion of unity." And of the cultural disintegration caused by British rule in India, Eliot wrote, "The cause lies in the fact that there can be no permanent compromise between the extremes of an external rule which is content to keep order and leave the social structure unaltered, and a complete cultural assimilation. The failure to arrive at the latter is a religious failure." *Notes towards the Definition of Culture,* pp. 157 and 167.

34. "Religion without Humanism," in *Humanism and America,* ed. Norman Foerster (New York: Farrar and Rinehart, 1930), p. 112.

a concrete organic society, supported by religious belief, that would allow for the accommodation of the individual and the social points of view. However, we must remember that this is an *ideal* solution (no one could be more conscious of *that* than Eliot), and in practice the problems remain.

There is one more aspect of Eliot's attitude toward personality that must be considered before the discussion can be considered complete, his attitude toward the concept of the soul. This changed radically during the course of his career. I believe this to be, in fact, the single most important change in his total view of the nature of things, though the effect of this change on his critical thought is not clearcut, direct, or immediately apparent. That, of course, would be much too simple!

The classical attitude recommended in Eliot's early criticism is literally so, in the sense that it contemplates a return to a strictly Aristotelian theory of the soul as against the Christian doctrine. In a philosophical essay of 1916, Eliot compared at length Aristotle's concept of the soul with that of Leibniz. Here is his statement of Aristotle's theory: "Soul is to body as cutting is to the axe: realizing itself in its actions, and not completely real when abstracted from what it does. . . . For Aristotle reality is here and now; and the true nature of mind is found in the activity which it exercises. Attempt to analyse the mind, as a thing, and it is nothing. It is an operation."[35] These sentences need no extended analysis; I have discussed above Eliot's objection to the assumptions of the psychologists, his argument that there is no "mind" substantial enough to contain "ideas." This is a sublime "objectivity," banishing to utter unreality all that is not *realized*, all "velleities and carefully caught

35. "The Development of Leibniz' Monadism," Appendix I of *Knowledge and Experience*, p. 195. This essay was reprinted from *The Monist* 26 (October 1916): 534–56.

regrets." For Leibniz, on the other hand, "the ego is substance."[36] Eliot discussed at some length the significance of
Leibniz's concept of the soul: "In this he shows again an
important difference between the ancient and the modern
world. It is illustrated in the prejudice of Aristotle against
the differences between individuals of the same species
which he ascribes to the perverse and unaccountable influence of matter. To the Greek, this variety of points of view
would seem a positive evil; as a theory of knowledge, it
would seem a refuge of scepticism; to Leibniz and the modern world, it enhances the interest of life."[37] Eliot was quite
definite in identifying the cause of Leibniz's interest in "the
differences between individuals"; it was Leibniz's "theological motive," or as Eliot put it later his "theological bias."[38]
This theological bias, Eliot makes quite plain, is Leibniz's
desire to remain orthodox in his doctrine of the personal
immortality of the soul: "Leibniz' theory of the soul is, like
that of Descartes, derived from scholasticism."[39]

We may press this discussion one step further. Eliot observed of Leibniz, "His orthodoxy is more alarming than
others' revolution."[40] He was referring to the fact that
Leibniz seemed to demonstrate that the scholastic doctrine
of the soul led, if its implications were pursued to their
logical conclusion, to the concept that each soul is a "win-
dowless" monad, that it is never acted upon by "external
forces" but contains from the beginning by a "pre-estab-
lished harmony" the principles of its own acting and suffer-
ing. "Hell is alone, the other figures in it / Merely projections."

Eliot suggested another result of Leibniz's theory that
"the ego is substance": "Hence a tendency to psycholo-

36. *Ibid.*, p. 182.
37. *Ibid.*, p. 191.
38. *Ibid.*, pp. 182 and 195.
39. *Ibid.*, p. 192.
40. "Leibniz' Monads and Bradley's Finite Centres," in *ibid.*, p. 198.

gism, to maintain that ideas always find their home in particular minds, that they have a psychological as well as a logical existence. Leibniz on this side opened the way for modern idealism."[41] This psychologism would be much the same thing as the representational theory of knowledge, which I have argued to be analogous to the concept of the dissociation of sensibility. In short, I do not think it too much to say that in the period represented by *The Sacred Wood* Eliot attributed partly to the influence of the Christian (or, to be more precise, the scholastic) doctrine of the soul many of the institutions of the modern mind that he deprecated: the cult of personality, subjective idealism, the dissociation of sensibility, and perhaps Romanticism. Comparing Aristotle and Leibniz, Eliot plainly expressed his own preference: "When [Leibniz] turns . . . to the immortality of the soul, we feel a certain repulsion; . . . we know that Aristotle and Plato were somehow more secure, better balanced, and less superstitious than the man who was in power of intellect their equal."[42] Again, "Aristotle was not embarrassed by a belief in personal immortality."[43] Of the literary essays of the early period, "Tradition and the Individual Talent" is the most Aristotelian. Here we may recall a sentence I have quoted before: "The point of view which I am struggling to attack is perhaps related to the metaphysical theory of the substantial unity of the soul: for my meaning is, that the poet has, not a 'personality' to express, but a particular medium."

The reader will have anticipated the question I am going to raise at this point. Did Eliot's acceptance of Christianity alter his attitude to the soul? This question suggests another: Is there an analogous revaluation of personality in Eliot's literary criticism? Leaving aside for now the second

41. "The Development of Leibniz' Monadism," in *ibid.*, p. 197.
42. *Ibid.*, p. 196.
43. *Ibid.*, p. 190.

question, I reply to the first that such a change is, in fact, one of the most important developments in Eliot's thought. I shall illustrate that development with several references. With the sentence from "Tradition and the Individual Talent" at the end of the previous paragraph, compare a sentence translated by Eliot from the French of Charles Maurron for the *Criterion* of September 1927: "It might seem, at least, rash to base any system whatever upon the indivisibility of the soul, evident for St. Thomas and for every Christian—very much more doubtful for us."[44] Two years later, in *Animula,* Eliot expressed the emotional equivalent of the scholastic philosophers' idea of the simple soul ("a simple substance and therefore incorruptible," in the concise formula of Stephen Dedalus). We should observe, however, that Eliot did not picture the encounter of the simple soul with "the imperatives of 'is and seems' / And may and may not" with the resoluteness of Dante before him: "Issues from the hand of time the simple soul / Irresolute and selfish, misshapen, lame, / Unable to fare forward or retreat." But the last paragraph of the *Four Quartets* sets as "the end of all our exploring . . . that which was the beginning; . . . A condition of complete simplicity."

There is a passage from 1935 that sums up twenty years of Eliot's thought about personality and about the individual and society. Eliot recalls and in a sense reaffirms the individualism of the early period, but only upon condition of the substantial unity of the soul:

> *La vie est un dépouillement*—I have quoted this phrase of Gourmont before now, and I think Ezra Pound quoted it before I did; and the phrase has a long history behind it; to be free we must be stripped, like the sea-god Glaucus, of any number of encrustations of education and frequentation; we must divest ourselves even of our ancestors. But to undertake this stripping of acquired ideas, we must make one assumption: that of

44. "Concerning 'Intuition,' " *The Criterion* 6 (September 1927): 232.

the individuality of each human being; we must, in fact, believe in the soul.[45]

The change in Eliot's attitude toward the soul outlined above did lead, I am convinced, to a change in his evaluation of the personal element in literature. However, I shall defer a discussion of that change to the chapter on Form. Here, what I want to emphasize is the limited nature of that change; it by no means caused a simple reversal of Eliot's critical position. In the later criticism, as in the earlier, Eliot would not willingly pardon in the poet "a deliberate attempt to express his personality." For at the end, as at the beginning, the great central theme of Eliot's criticism is to affirm the primacy of the aim "to see the object as in itself it really is." That is a goal never, of course, to be completely realized, for the way to it is escape from the self, and "Humility is endless."

It is to be observed, in fact, that Eliot's most violent attack on personality in literature was made *after* his conversion, in *After Strange Gods.* There he seems to hint that the increasingly greater degree of expression of personality in modern literature is the work of the Devil.[46] But there is a crucial distinction to be noted: Eliot's concern there was for the *personality of the reader;* he objected to writers who attempted "to impose upon their readers their own *personal view* of life."[47]

It seems to be commonly agreed among interpreters of Eliot that one of the personal problems lying behind his critical and creative work is that of the difficulty, in the modern world, of *belief.* But, if permitted to reach for the forbidden fruit of interpretation, I should be tempted, not quite to reverse this formula, but to look at the problem

45. "Notes on the Way," *Time and Tide* 16 (January 19, 1935): 89.

46. *After Strange Gods* (New York: Harcourt, Brace and Company, 1934), pp. 57–62.

47. *Ibid.,* p. 57.

from a different angle. It seems to be equally true to say that the personal problem that may be read between the lines of Eliot's criticism is too great credulity, or, more precisely, susceptibility to influence by powerful literary personalities. In fact, *influence* is too weak a word here; the one Eliot used is *possession*, with more than a hint of a metaphor drawn from demonology. (Perhaps we should interpret the reference, in *After Strange Gods*, to the work of the Devil as an extension of this metaphor of "possession.") When I speak here of a personal problem, I do not refer to the mature Eliot, but to a period of adolescence. In the "Note on the Development of Taste in Poetry," Eliot frankly stated that he was "generalising [his] own history." "At this period [i.e., 'until my nineteenth or twentieth year'], the poem, or the poetry of a single poet, invades the youthful consciousness and assumes complete possession for a time. . . . It is not deliberate choice of a poet to mimic, but writing under a kind of daemonic possession by one poet."[48] *After Strange Gods* seems to have been almost universally deprecated, and I do not quarrel with that judgment. However, I think it must be admitted that Eliot there (and elsewhere) put his finger on a real problem. Those who have not experienced it directly themselves have probably noted it in others. I have known an excellent student of literature to reject modern literature with almost puritanical fervor, in reaction against just the kind of "possession" Eliot speaks of.

But it is not for the diagnosis of the problem but for its radical solution that *After Strange Gods* deserves rebuke. Three years later Eliot formulated a more temperate solution: "Wide reading . . . is valuable because in the process of being affected by one powerful personality after another, we cease to be dominated by any one, or by any small number. The very different views of life, cohabiting in our minds, affect each other, and our own personality asserts

48. *The Use of Poetry*, 2nd ed. (London: Faber and Faber, 1964), p. 34.

itself and gives each a place in some arrangement peculiar to ourself."[49] It is instructive to compare with these sentences the famous one from "Tradition and the Individual Talent": "The progress of an artist is a continual self-sacrifice, a continual extinction of personality."[50]

Finally, we should note that throughout his critical career Eliot made a number of considered statements about the personal element in poetry, statements that almost certainly refer implicitly to "Tradition and the Individual Talent" (whether to correct it or to guard against misinterpretation of it, we may leave an open question). One of the best known of these statements occurs in the essay on Yeats in *On Poetry and Poets*. I shall quote two less accessible essays. In 1924 Eliot remarked of Valéry's poetry that "it is impersonal in the sense that personal emotion, personal experience, is extended and completed in something impersonal—not in the sense of something divorced from personal experience and passion. No good poetry is the latter."[51] In 1931 Eliot made what I believe we may take as a definitive statement of his views on personality in literature (it is also a good summary of the material of this chapter): "Browning . . . is perhaps *too* objective, without having that large and intricate pattern which objectivity requires: Donne, Corbière, Laforgue begin with their own feelings, and their limitation is that they do not always get much outside or beyond; Shakespeare, one feels, arrives at an objective world by a process from himself, whoever he was, as the centre and starting point; but too often, one thinks with Browning, here is a world with no particular interesting man inside it, no consistent point of view."[52]

49. "Religion and Literature," *Selected Essays*, p. 349.

50. *The Sacred Wood*, p. 53, and *Selected Essays*, p. 7.

51. "A Brief Introduction to the Method of Paul Valéry," in Paul Valéry, *Le Serpent*, trans. Mark Wardle (London: R. Cobden-Sanderson, 1924), p. 14.

52. "Donne in Our Time," *A Garland for John Donne* ed. Theodore Spencer (Cambridge: Harvard University Press, 1931), pp. 15–16.

6
Form

No one definition is adequate to cover all of Eliot's uses of the word *form,* for they range from the most limited and conventional technical sense to those that seem to be intuitive rather than discursive: "Only by the form, the pattern / Can words or music reach / The stillness." For *Form* appears to hold the central position in Eliot's criticism that *Imagination* held in Romantic criticism. The use of the word in an absolute sense is a striking feature of Eliot's thought: "I am accustomed to the search for form: but Kipling never seems to be searching for form, but only for a particular form for each poem."[1] Note that *form* here is not simply a collective term for *particular forms.*

a. Form and Content

Eliot recognizes the conventional distinction between form and content. But this conventional distinction acquires a unique meaning as it takes its place in Eliot's critical thought. Eliot wrote that "influence can be exerted through form, whereas one makes disciples only among

1. "Rudyard Kipling," *On Poetry and Poets* (New York: Farrar, Straus and Giroux, 1961), p. 277.

those who sympathize with the content."[2] (Compare this sentence with the passage from Arnold quoted at the beginning of the second part of chapter 1.) In this sentence, content appears to mean the poet's philosophy, or better, "view of life," and form everything else. The special meaning that the distinction of form and content has for Eliot lies in its correspondence with his distinction between the individual and the social points of view. Content corresponds to the individual point of view, and the need for form is recognized when the poet takes account of the social point of view.

Before this discussion of form and content is complete, it will lead us into a consideration of the poet's relation to a *specific* social order. But at present I am using the term *the social point of view* in the absolute sense already defined: the point of view from which the individual is forced to realize that his "world" is not "the world one and impersonal" but only one of many possible points of view. It is the situation, in other words, in which the individual is presented with the choice between pyrrhonism and belief.

The sentence in the last paragraph but one, which I have taken for my text, occurs in an essay in which Eliot weighs the strength (the technical excellence) and weakness (the fantastic and eccentric philosophy) of the *Cantos* of Pound, an essay with the significant title, "Isolated Superiority." In it Eliot confesses that "I am seldom interested in what he is saying, but only in the way he says it." But he continues immediately, "That does not mean that he is saying nothing; for ways of saying nothing are not interesting. Swinburne's form is uninteresting, because he is literally saying next to nothing, and unless you mean something with your words they will do nothing for you."[3]

At the opposite extreme from Eliot's attitude to the po-

2. "Isolated Superiority," *The Dial* 84 (January 1928): 4.
3. *Ibid.*, p. 6.

etry of Pound would be his attitude to the poetry of Dante, of which he said, "But if you yourself are convinced of a certain view of life, then you irresistibly and inevitably believe that if any one else comes to 'understand' it fully, his understanding *must* terminate in belief."[4] Between these two extremes—they are rather theoretical limits than actualities—of "pure poetry" and higher propaganda, Eliot locates the varying degrees of belief with which different readers can respond to different poems. In 1941 Eliot, contrasting his method with that of Kipling, remarked, "I know of no writer of such great gifts for whom poetry seems to have been more purely an instrument. Most of us are interested in the form for its own sake—not apart from the content, but because we aim at making something which shall first of all *be*, something which in consequence will have the capability of exciting, within a limited range, a considerable variety of responses from different readers. For Kipling the poem is something which is intended to *act*."[5]

We must recognize that for Eliot all worthwhile poets do desire "to impose upon their readers their own *personal view* of life," or at least the "natural man" in the poet desires this. But this propagandist intention is legitimate, for Eliot, only if the poet has translated his personal view of life into its objective correlative, and this in practice implies, for Eliot, some traditional belief, like Dante's scholastic Christianity, which "has reached the point of immediate acceptance, when it has become almost a physical modification."[6] In this last sentence Eliot appears to be trying to suggest the development of the unified sensibility by way of an analogy with the concept of evolutionary adaptation.

At the end of the previous chapter, we observed that

4. "Dante," *Selected Essays*, 2nd ed. (New York: Harcourt, Brace and World, 1960), p. 230.
5. "Rudyard Kipling," *On Poetry and Poets*, p. 277.
6. "Dante," *The Sacred Wood*, 2nd ed. (London: Methuen, 1960), pp. 162–63.

Eliot's criticism of writers who attempt to impose their
personal view of life was in the end justified by his concern
for the *personality* of the reader. Short of its full religious
meaning, discipleship is for Eliot a degrading relationship.
Not only that, it alienates the disciple from *his* reality, which
can be for him, in Eliot's view, the only *reality:* "It is simply
not true that works of fiction, prose or verse . . . *directly*
extend our knowledge of life. Direct knowledge of life is
knowledge directly in relation to ourselves, it is our knowledge of *how* people behave in general, of *what* they are like
in general, in so far as that part of life in which we ourselves
have participated gives us material for generalization."[7]
This is a perfect expression, in the year 1935, of the idealism of Eliot's thesis, applied to literary criticism.

In fact, if we recall here that one of the basic concepts
upon which Eliot's thesis and his early criticism are based
is that of the impenetrability of points of view, we perceive
the real reason for the absolute necessity for form, in the
sense of the word I am now examining. If, in reading a play
of Shakespeare, we orient ourselves toward the experience
of Shakespeare rather than toward the play, we are simply
grasping at a shadow.

We can, in fact, take a much more extreme example than
that of a reader of a Shakespearean play to elicit the significance of form. Let us take the poet of the "first voice," who
is concerned "only with finding the right words or, anyhow,
the least wrong words. He is not concerned whether anybody else will ever listen to them or not, or whether anybody else will ever understand them if he does." For even
a poet of the first voice cannot escape the social point of
view, engaging, as he must, with the language: "There is
first, [Gottfried Benn] says, an inert embryo or 'creative
germ' *[ein dumpfer schöpferischer Keim]* and, on the other
hand, the Language, the resources of the words at the

7. "Religion and Literature," *Selected Essays*, p. 349.

poet's command. He has something germinating in him for which he must find words; but he cannot know what words he wants until he has found the words; he cannot identify this embryo until it has been transformed into an arrangement of the right words in the right order. When you have the words for it, the 'thing' for which the words had to be found has disappeared, replaced by a poem."[8] Four pages later, Eliot resumes this same topic but uses the terms "form and material," and there the last sentence above becomes "finally the material is identified with its form." In short, the poet can communicate with himself, if I may put it so, only through "form." However much the passage quoted owes to Gottfried Benn, it is an almost perfect application to literary criticism of Bradley's concept of "immediate experience," or "the silence" as Eliot might call it. The act of knowledge, according to Bradley, is the identity of subject and object, and this act *precedes* consciousness. But when we become conscious, knowledge falls apart into subject and object, for we become conscious when we are aware of other possible points of view upon the object. Real knowledge is absolutely private—*immediate* experience—and yet we can only be aware of that knowledge as *mediated* by the terms of subject and object, in other words, in the social world. We can, in short, only know reality if we find its objective correlative.

Form, then, is not simply a poet's deliberate "compromise" with the social point of view. A man who could sustain absolute belief in his individual point of view would be a mystic and not a poet—he would be, in the terms of Yeats's analysis of subjectivity and objectivity, Saint or Fool. The highest model that the poet could follow is Pascal, who united "the profoundest scepticism with the deepest faith." In 1935 Eliot observed that "the Church offers today the last asylum for one type of mind which the Middle

8. "The Three Voices of Poetry," *On Poetry and Poets,* pp. 106–7.

Ages would hardly have expected to find among the faithful: that of the sceptic."[9] (This remark comes from an essay
in which Eliot considered the increasing pressures on the
writer to commit himself to some secular faith, such as
Communism or Fascism.)

The distinction of form and content, then, does not yield
a negative definition of form. The search for form, the
maintenance of the critical, the sceptical attitude together
with belief results in "substantial human emotions, such
emotions as observation can confirm." But there are passages in Eliot's criticism where the interaction of the poet's
individual point of view with the social point of view is
described as contributing to the search for form in a way
that is by comparison positive. In these passages Eliot gives
specific content to the social point of view; this theme
comes to a point when Eliot considers the relationship of
Shakespeare to his audience in the Elizabethan playhouse.
The development of the cinema helped, by contrast, to
focus Eliot's attention on one of the essentials of the thea-
ter or the music hall: "The working man who went to the
music-hall and saw Marie Lloyd and joined in the chorus
was himself performing part of the act; he was engaged in
that collaboration of the audience with the artist which is
necessary in all art and most obviously in dramatic art. He
will now go to the cinema."[10] This was written in 1922,
before the development of the talking film, but this does
not affect the distinction that Eliot had in mind. In 1936 he
again made a comparison of the essential capabilities of the
cinema and of the stage: "When we see a great music-hall
comedian on the stage, such as George Robey or Ernie

9. "Notes on the Way," *Time and Tide* 16 (January 5, 1935): 6. Eliot continued,
"Obviously, I mean by the sceptic, the man who suspects the origins of his own
beliefs, as well as those of others; who is most suspicious of those which are most
passionately held . . . ; who suspects other people's motives because he has
learned the deceitfulness of his own."
10. "Marie Lloyd," *Selected Essays*, p. 407.

Lotinga, we feel that he is conscious of his audience, that a great deal of the effect depends upon a sympathy set up between actor and audience."[11]

In the essay "The Possibility of a Poetic Drama," Eliot discussed the dramatist's difficulties in "a formless age" like the present. Explaining why Shakespeare, in contrast, was "very fortunate," Eliot used an interesting metaphor drawn from Aristotle, which defines the response of the audience as the half-formed matter, the potentiality, that made possible the great dramatic form of the Elizabethans: "To create a form is not merely to invent a shape, a rhyme or rhythm. . . . The *framework* which was provided for the Elizabethan dramatist was not merely blank verse and the five-act play and the Elizabethan playhouse. . . . It was also the half-formed ὑλή [*sic*], the 'temper of the age' (an unsatisfactory phrase), a preparedness, a habit on the part of the public, to respond to particular stimuli. There is a book to be written on the commonplaces of any great dramatic period, the handling of Fate or Death, the recurrence of mood, tone, situation."[12] This theme appears again in "A Dialogue on Dramatic Poetry."

But it is not just any responsive, collaborating audience that Eliot desired, but "one which could cut across all the present stratifications of public taste—stratifications which are perhaps a sign of social disintegration."[13] In "The Possibility of a Poetic Drama" Eliot criticized the drama of Claudel and Maeterlinck and other drama based on a philosophy, an "idea-emotion," in "the attempt to supply the defect of structure by an internal structure," simply by quoting Butcher's translation of the *Poetics:* "But most important of all is the structure of the incidents. For Tragedy is an imitation, not of men, but of an action and of life, and

11. "The Need for Poetic Drama," *The Listener* 16 (November 25, 1936): 994.
12. *The Sacred Wood,* pp. 63–64.
13. *The Use of Poetry,* 2nd ed. (London: Faber and Faber, 1964), p. 153.

life consists in action, and its end is a mode of action, not a quality." Eliot's intent here is rather obscure, though some light is cast on it at the end of the essay, where he suggests that the modern dramatist begins at the "wrong end" when he aims "at the small public which wants 'poetry'" and recommends instead starting with "a form of entertainment," such as the music hall.[14]

The theme of "The Possibility of a Poetic Drama" becomes clearer when compared with a review, written a few months earlier, of a poetic drama by J. M. Murry: "Mr. Murry cannot escape an audience—comparatively small and comparatively cultivated—which has no dramatic habits, but desires to share, to destroy his solitude. . . . He is not held down by the necessity of *entertaining* an audience cruder than himself; the emotional structure is the only structure. In a dramatic structure the minor emotions, or the emotions of the minor characters, are related to the major emotions through the actions."[15] These reflections culminate in a passage written in 1933 on the "several levels of significance" in the plays of Shakespeare: "For the simplest auditors there is the plot, for the more thoughtful the character and conflict of character, for the more literary the words and phrasing, for the more musically sensitive the rhythm, and for auditors of greater sensitiveness and understanding a meaning which reveals itself gradually. And I do not believe that the classification of audience is so clear-cut as this; but rather that the sensitiveness of every auditor is acted upon by all these elements at once, though in different degrees of consciousness."[16]

I observe in this connection that it may be well to modify what is probably the usual interpretation of the second section of "The Game of Chess" ("when Lil's husband got

14. *The Sacred Wood,* pp. 67 and 70.
15. "The Poetic Drama," *The Athenaeum* (May 14, 1920), p. 635.
16. *The Use of Poetry,* p. 153.

demobbed, I said . . ."): that the moral decadence in "low" life equals that in "high" life. A careful reading of the essay on Marie Lloyd suggests a rather different interpretation. There Eliot said, "I have called her the expressive figure of the lower classes. There is no such expressive figure for any other class. The middle classes have no such idol: the middle classes are morally corrupt. That is to say, their own life fails to find a Marie Lloyd to express it."[17] In fact, I suspect that this section of *The Waste Land* was suggested by a routine of Marie Lloyd's.

Eliot went so far as to say that "I myself should like an audience which could neither read nor write."[18] Here I think he can be seen to approximate what I take to be the half-conscious theme of the English comic tradition from Chaucer onwards. The attitude of English comedy is, if not quite the contrary of the aristocratic rigor of the Aristotelian theory, at least quite different. Aristotle says, "Comedy represents the worse types of men . . . in the sense that the ridiculous is a species of ugliness or badness."[19] The theme of the English comic tradition attains conscious expression at least as early as Book XIV, chapter 1 of *Tom Jones*, in which Fielding prepares the reader for the high society of London: "What Mr. Pope says of women is very applicable to most in this station, who are, indeed, so entirely made up of form and affectation, that they have no character at all, at least none which appears. . . . The various callings in the lower spheres produce the great variety of humorous characters." It is perhaps best not to interpret even Ben Jonson as a "classical" exception; observe his tribute to Sir Ralph Shelton, "That to the vulgar canst thyself apply, / Treading a better path, not contrary" (Epigram CXIX). By the time we get to Joyce and Faulkner, the

17. "Marie Lloyd," *Selected Essays*, p. 407.
18. *The Use of Poetry*, p. 152.
19. *The Poetics*, chap. 5, in *Classical Literary Criticism*, trans. T. S. Dorsch (Baltimore: Penguin Books, 1965), p. 37.

significance of the intellectual's contemplation of "low" life —his reliance on the people for "form"—becomes virtually an explicit theme. The overall structure of *Ulysses* is that of Wordsworth's "Resolution and Independence."

This aspect of Eliot's literary criticism is analogous to his attempt in *Notes towards the Definition of Culture* to rectify the "impression of thinness which Arnold's 'culture' conveys to a modern reader," which, he said, "is partly due to the absence of social background to his picture." Eliot insisted that "the culture of the individual cannot be isolated from that of the group, and that the culture of the group cannot be abstracted from that of the whole society."[20] Arnold's conception of Culture is in the tradition of the eighteenth century, the Enlightenment, while Eliot's, though not repudiating that tradition, supplements it from the work of the anthropologists of the late nineteenth and of the twentieth centuries. It is relevant to recall here Eliot's criticism of Babbitt and his followers for failing to leave a place "not only for the mob, but (what is more important) for the mob part of the mind in themselves."

The argument begun above has now come full circle. We have considered two points: the necessity for action in drama, and the advantages of writing for an audience that includes the lower classes as well as the upper. For Eliot, at least, these two ideas are connected: it is in writing for the people that a *poet* is forced to supply the *dramatic* element of the poetic drama. But there is one link missing in the argument; to answer the question "Why must there be action in the drama?" we have so far done no more than observe in passing the famous statement from Aristotle's *Poetics:* "Life consists in action, and its end is a mode of action, not a quality." The entire meaning of this sentence is perhaps not immediately obvious. The best commentary on it that I have found is a paragraph from the *Nicomachean*

20. *Christianity and Culture,* pp. 94 and 96.

Ethics. In fact, I can think of no better commentary on the tenor of *Eliot's* early poetry and criticism than the following words:

> It makes, perhaps, no small difference whether we place the chief good in possession [of virtue] or in use, in state of mind or in activity. For the state of mind may exist without producing any good result, as in a man who is asleep or in some other way quite inactive. . . . As in the Olympic Games it is not the most beautiful and the strongest that are crowned but those who compete (for it is some of these that are victorious), so those who act win, and rightly win, the noble and good things in life."[21]

So far we have been examining the function and the significance of form rather than the *nature* of form. It will be the purpose of the next section of this chapter to search for a more specific answer to the question of *what* form is.

b. Form as Self-Consistency

Eliot often suggested in his early criticism that sensation and logic are the two basic functions of the mind. We may be tempted to end our search for the definition of form right here with the apparently satisfying answer that sensation is or provides the matter of poetry, and logic is or provides the form. (By "formal logic" I do not mean, of course, the actual use of the syllogism but, in a general sense, the "logic of consistency," the science of the form of our knowledge.) In the end we shall find that this answer is somewhat too simple, but there is no doubt that it takes us a good way in the right direction. Eliot's concept of form is clearly analogous to the "Coherence Theory of Truth"

21. 1098b32–1099a6, *The Works of Aristotle,* ed. W. D. Ross, 12 vols. (Oxford: Oxford University Press, 1908–52), 9: n. pag.

in philosophy. The key words in Eliot's criticism that reflect the influence of this theory are *consistency, coherence, logic, simplification* (in the sense of "making one"), and *system.* Eliot's definition of form is implied in the following sentences: "Since Kyd . . . there has been no form to arrest, so to speak, the flow of spirit at any particular point before it expands and ends its course in the desert of exact likeness to the reality which is perceived by the most commonplace mind. . . . In [the Elizabethans'] plays there are faults of inconsistency, faults of incoherency."[22]

Often we meet the very language of logic: "The world of Swinburne . . . has the necessary completeness and self-sufficiency for justification and permanence. . . . The deductions are true to the postulates."[23] We are told that "Jonson's characters conform to the logic of the emotions of their world. It is a world like Lobatchevsky's; the worlds created by artists like Jonson are like systems of non-Euclidean geometry."[24] This criterion of consistency holds beyond the level of the single work: "A man might, hypothetically, compose any number of fine passages or even of whole poems which would each give satisfaction, and yet not be a great poet, unless we felt them to be united by one significant, consistent, and developing personality."[25] The criterion rises finally, of course, above the level of the individual talent to "the form of European, of English literature."

But the definition of form as logic or self-consistency is not entirely adequate. Even a casual reader of Eliot will probably have a vague impression that the word *form* as he used it conveys a feeling of solidity; perhaps to say that it

22. "Four Elizabethan Dramatists," *Selected Essays,* p. 93.
23. "Swinburne as Poet," *The Sacred Wood,* p. 149 and *Selected Essays,* pp. 284–85.
24. "Ben Jonson," *The Sacred Wood,* pp. 116–17, and *Selected Essays,* p. 135; the last sentence was omitted here.
25. "John Ford," *Selected Essays,* p. 179.

has a "third dimension" is to use the right metaphor. This is suggested by the phrase *shape without form* from "The Hollow Men." In an early essay Eliot speaks of the poet as "impelled . . . by a desire to give form to something in his mind."[26] We find in this idiom the precise "feel" the word had for him. If we recall at this point the import of the first section of this chapter—on the distinction of form and content—I think we can understand why this is so. The poet's content comes from within; it is his personal point of view, ultimately his "immediate experience." To give it form is to find—the objective correlative. Just above we examined a passage dealing with the poet of the "first voice," in which form virtually came to be the same thing as the poem itself. *Form* is the central term in Eliot's criticism, and as with *Imagination* in Romantic criticism there is a tendency for it to swallow the other terms. We shall have to recognize this tendency as intuitively true to Eliot's critical view, and on the other hand, for the purposes of discursive analysis, we must resist it.

It is interesting to note that this sense of the solidity of the word *form* in Eliot's writing corresponds to Hegel's definition of Classic Form as "a perfect harmony between the idea as spiritual individuality, and the form as sensuous and corporal reality." It is even more relevant to notice that it corresponds to Aristotle's analysis, which recognizes neither form nor matter separately as substantial, but rather their union. In short, Eliot's concept of form is what is sometimes called "organic form."

I now return to a further analysis of self-consistency as an aspect of form; the object is to find the reason why "it is essential that a work of art should be self-consistent."[27] The complete text of Eliot's remarks on Swinburne, from which fragments were given earlier, is apt for this purpose:

26. "The Poetic Drama," *The Athenaeum* (May 14, 1920), p. 635.
27. "Four Elizabethan Dramatists," *Selected Essays*, p. 93.

It might seem to be intimated, by what has been said, that the work of Swinburne can be shown to be a sham, just as bad verse is a sham. It would only be so if you could produce or suggest something that it pretends to be and is not. The world of Swinburne does not depend upon some other world which it simulates; it has the necessary completeness and self-suffi-ciency for justification and permanence. It is impersonal, and no one else could have made it. The deductions are true to the postulates.[28]

It is self-consistency, then, that separates the poem from, makes it independent of, "reality" ("some other world which it simulates") on the one hand, and the poet ("it is impersonal") on the other. If it be asked *why* the poem should be independent of reality and of the poet, we need only recall the concept of the absoluteness of the individual point of view set forth in Eliot's thesis. There *is* no "exter-nal" world independent of points of view, and any individ-ual point of view is impenetrable by another. To seek to escape in either of these directions is "vanity and a striving after wind." It is to get "further and further away from the poem without arriving at any other destination."[29] In fact, the second sentence in the passage above is an exact ap-plication of an argument, in Eliot's thesis, that his concept of the point of view does not amount to solipsism: "A world which is built up from the subject's point of view . . . is [his] only world, but it is not a solipsistic world, for it is not contrasted with any other possible world" [i.e., an "exter-nal world"].[30] The whole passage is an exact application of

28. "Swinburne as Poet," *The Sacred Wood*, p. 149, and *Selected Essays*, pp. 284–85.

29. "The Three Voices of Poetry," *On Poetry and Poets*, p. 108.

30. *Knowledge and Experience* (New York: Farrar, Straus and Company, 1964), p. 44. Compare: "[Jonson's verse] is what it is; it does not pretend to be another thing. . . . We cannot call a man's work superficial when it is the creation of a world; a man cannot be accused of dealing superficially with the world which he himself has created; the superficies *is* the world." "Ben Jonson," *The Sacred Wood*, p. 116.

the Coherence Theory of Truth to literary criticism. The phrase *completeness and self-sufficiency* echoes the two qualities —coherence and comprehensiveness—that according to Bradley make up the "test of system," which is the criterion by which we define truth.[31]

Elsewhere Eliot used the phrase "self-subsistent reality" to describe this independence of the work of art that results from its coherence.[32] By contrast, "Goethe's demon inevitably sends us back to Goethe."[33] (Compare the sentence from Johnson's *Preface to Shakespeare:* "The composition refers us only to the writer; we pronounce the name of *Cato*, but we think on *Addison.*") As for the relation of the work of art to reality, Eliot wrote, "I object . . . to the interpretation, and I would have a work of art such that it needs only to be completed and cannot be altered by each interpretation. . . . The closer a play is built upon real life, the more the performance by one actor will differ from another, and the more the performances of one generation of actors will differ from those of the next."[34] In other words, the poem must not depend on order and meaning assumed to exist in the "real" world (or, in the mind of the poet); the organization must be gotten out into the poem. It must *be* a world, not refer to a world.

But we must avoid a misunderstanding at this point. The independence of the work of art is not to be interpreted to mean that it has no connection with what we take to be reality. That would be a meaningless idea. Eliot's position is well expressed in these sentences: "Characters should be real in relation to our own life, certainly, as even a very minor character of Shakespeare may be real; but they must also be real in relation to each other; and the closeness of emotional pattern in the latter way is an important part of

31. *Essays on Truth and Reality* (Oxford: Clarendon Press, 1914), p. 202.
32. "Cyril Tourneur," *Selected Essays*, p. 162.
33. "The Possibility of a Poetic Drama," *The Sacred Wood*, p. 66.
34. "Four Elizabethan Dramatists," *Selected Essays*, p. 96.

dramatic merit. The personages of Tourneur have . . . this togetherness. . . . Hence the whole action . . . has its own self-subsistent reality."[35] Note, in the first sentence, the significance of Eliot's use of the phrase "our own life" rather than "reality."

Similarly, the independence of the work of art in relation to the artist is not to be interpreted as impersonality in the sense of "something divorced from personal experience and passion. No good poetry is the latter."[36] Even of Ben Jonson, whose work seldom attracts biographical interpretations, Eliot wrote, "His type of personality found its relief in something falling under the category of burlesque or farce. . . . The simplification consists largely in reduction of detail, in the seizing of aspects relevant to the relief of an emotional impulse."[37] This last sentence recalls Eliot's comment, in the essay on Hamlet, about the artist's "ability to intensify the world to his emotions."[38]

Finally, this is the proper place for some observations on the form of poetry as a whole—"the form of European, of English literature"—and on "the relation of the work of art to art, of the work of literature to literature, of 'criticism' to criticism."[39] A great deal could be written under this topic about the relation of the individual talent to tradition. Instead, we may go straight to the heart of the matter by seeing it as what Eliot in 1928 defined as the central theme of *The Sacred Wood:* "the problem of the integrity of poetry, with the repeated assertion that when we are considering poetry we must consider it primarily as poetry and not another thing."[40] This sentence sets forth the essential pur-

35. "Cyril Tourneur," *Selected Essays*, p. 162.
36. "A Brief Introduction to the Method of Paul Valéry," in Paul Valéry, *Le Serpent,* trans. Mark Wardle (London: R. Cobden-Sanderson, 1924), p. 14.
37. "Ben Jonson," *The Sacred Wood*, p. 120, and *Selected Essays*, pp. 137–38.
38. "Hamlet and His Problems," *The Sacred Wood*, p. 102, and *Selected Essays*, p. 126.
39. "The Function of Criticism," *Selected Essays*, pp. 12, 14.
40. "Preface to the 1928 Edition," *The Sacred Wood*, p. viii.

pose of Eliot's long critical battle against the concepts of the function of literature professed by Arnold and I. A. Richards, those fostered by the example of Sainte-Beuve, and those engendered less directly by the influence of such men as Marx and Freud. And this sentence explains Eliot's high regard for the criticism of the seventeenth and eighteenth centuries, less "profound" in many ways than later criticism. Explaining why we should regard Dryden as "the *normal* critic," Eliot wrote, "A great merit of Dryden as a critic and as a critical influence is that he never transgresses the line beyond which the criticism of poetry becomes something else."[41]

But we must not oversimplify Eliot's position. In the 1928 "Preface" to *The Sacred Wood,* Eliot also confessed to "having passed on to another problem not touched upon in this book: that of the relation of poetry to the spiritual and social life of its time and of other times." A few years later he recognized that "all human affairs are involved with each other, that consequently all history involves abstraction, and that in attempting to win a full understanding of the poetry of a period you are led to the consideration of subjects which at first sight appear to have little bearing upon poetry."[42] The central concern of *The Use of Poetry,* from which these words are taken, is to mediate between this truth on the one hand and the integrity of poetry on the other. Eliot never reveals the influence of Bradley more clearly than in this recognition of the interconnection of all things balanced by insistence on the necessity for limiting a specific field of discourse so that it may possess internal coherence and form. The following sentences are a perfect expression in abstract and general form of Eliot's position: "In the common mind all interests are confused, and each degraded by the confusion. And

41. "Dryden the Critic, Defender of Sanity," *The Listener* 5 (April 29, 1931): 725.
42. *The Use of Poetry,* p. 76.

where they are confused, they cannot be related; in the common mind any specialised activity is conceived as something isolated from life, an odious task or a pastime of mandarins. To maintain the autonomy, and the disinterestedness, of every human activity, and to perceive it in relation to every other, require a considerable discipline."[43]

Eliot did not deny the value of the "heretical" schools of criticism, but rather affirmed that "there is a philosophic borderline, which you must not transgress too far or too often, if you wish to preserve your standing as a critic, and are not prepared to present yourself as a philosopher, metaphysician, sociologist, or psychologist instead."[44] But however much Eliot was concerned with the possible effect of these heresies on the *reading* of the literature of the past, with their tendency, that is, to get "further and further away from the poem without arriving at any other destination," he was probably more disturbed by the temptations they offered to, and by the burdens they placed upon, practicing poets. Therefore he continued to insist that "so long as poetry . . . [is] written, its first purpose must always be what it has always been—to give a peculiar kind of pleasure which has something constant in it throughout the ages, however difficult and various our explanations of that pleasure may be."[45] This is the primary reason for the imperative relationship of the individual talent to tradition, for the "necessity that he shall conform."

Eliot's concern that poetry remain true to itself does not mean that it has no truth in relation to what is beyond it. In his late criticism, at least, he wished to affirm a relationship between the form of poetry and the form of the universe. In 1951 he asserted that "it is ultimately the function

43. "The Function of a Literary Review," *The Criterion* 1 (July 1923): 421. This brief essay is a statement of principles made at the end of the first volume of *The Criterion*.
44. *The Use of Poetry*, p. 64.
45. "Experiment in Criticism," *The Bookman* 70 (November 1929): 232.

of art, in imposing a credible order upon ordinary reality, and thereby eliciting some perception of an order *in* reality, to bring us to a condition of serenity, stillness, and reconciliation."[46] It will be our next concern to analyze further the means by which the work of art achieves self-consistency and so imposes a credible order upon *ordinary reality*.

c. Form as Technique and Form as Convention

Form defined as self-consistency—a definition more or less peculiar to Eliot—is closely connected with form in the more common sense as a collective term for various techniques of art; and these two meanings of form are again closely related to form defined as convention, whether "of subject matter, of treatment, of verse or of dramatic form, of general philosophy of life."[47] The most concentrated discussions of the interdependency of these distinguishable senses of the word *form* occur in two essays of the middle period, "Four Elizabethan Dramatists" of 1924 and "A Dialogue on Dramatic Poetry" of 1928. In the former Eliot wrote,

> The great vice of English drama from Kyd to Galsworthy has been that its aim of realism was unlimited. . . . There has been no form to arrest, so to speak, the flow of spirit at any particular point before it expands and ends its course in the desert of exact likeness to the reality which is perceived by the most commonplace mind. . . . [The] great weakness [of the Elizabethans] is the same weakness as that of modern drama, it is the lack of a convention. . . . It is essential that a work of art should be self-consistent, that an artist should consciously or unconsciously draw a circle beyond which he does not trespass: on the one hand actual life is always the material, and on the other hand an abstraction from actual

46. "Poetry and Drama," *On Poetry and Poets*, p. 94.
47. "Four Elizabethan Dramatists," *Selected Essays*, p. 93.

life is a necessary condition to the creation of the work of art.[48]

I recommend that the reader compare this passage with the comments of John Dewey on Bradley quoted in chapter 1. The terms *ordinary reality* and *form* (Dewey is talking about Bradley's use of self-consistency as the criterion of truth) are almost exactly the same in both passages, as is the idea of form operating on ordinary reality to produce a "higher" reality, though of course Dewey's valuation of these ideas is quite different from Eliot's.

Before passing on to a discussion of technique, I shall indicate briefly the importance of convention in Eliot's critical view. In his thesis Eliot states flatly that "reality is a convention."[49] He does not mean here Reality as regarded by metaphysics, for that would be Reality from the Absolute point of view, reconciling all individual points of view into a harmonious whole. But for any finite point of view such reconciliation is impossible, for "the world, as we have seen, exists only as it is found in the experiences of finite centres, experiences so mad and strange that they will be boiled away before you boil them down to one homogeneous mass."[50] For us, then, the world seen from the social point of view is intractably inconsistent, and there can be no convention—in the sense of a coming together of points of view—except through convention—in the sense of a more or less arbitrary "abstraction of actual life." The alternative would be a reduction of reality to a sort of lowest common denominator, "the reality which is perceived by the most commonplace mind."

Before engaging with technique as an aspect of form, we may pursue further the question of Eliot's attitude to "ordinary reality" upon which form is to be imposed. It is impor-

48. *Ibid.*
49. *Knowledge and Experience,* p. 98.
50. *Ibid.,* p. 168.

tant not to overemphasize the distinction between Eliot and Dewey (or a corresponding position in literary theory). Eliot is, as Dewey said of Bradley, at a "half-way house." Eliot's reaction against imagination as it operated in late Romantic poetry led to an emphasis, comparatively speaking, on realism. More specifically, his distaste for Georgian poetry helped him to perceive "the poetical possibilities . . . of the more sordid aspects of the modern metropolis."[51] Here we touch upon one of the most significant themes in Eliot's criticism, one that can best be illustrated with some remarks that he made about Dryden and Baudelaire, poets whom Eliot compared in his first essay on Dryden.

A central theme can be traced through Eliot's several essays on Dryden; he attempted, each time more successfully, to formulate an alternative to the nineteenth-century view that Dryden was "unpoetic." In 1921 he began somewhat on the defensive, admitting that "Dryden has sunk by the persons he has elevated to distinction."[52] But by 1930 he had achieved nothing short of a transvaluation of the concept of "pure poetry": "Now, satire is one of the most difficult forms of poetry. . . . It must deal with matter which is by hypothesis unpoetic, and it must make that matter into poetry. And in this way satire is one of the most abstract branches of poetry; it is when successful a triumph of form; it is as near to that abstraction called pure poetry as any poetry can be."[53](We can see here why Eliot so often cited Dryden and Pope as "tests of catholic appreciation of poetry," of the appreciation, that is, of the poetic operation itself, since the reader is not seduced by conventionally "poetic" material: "I once said something to the effect that no person of our time can be said to know what poetry is

51. "What Dante Means to Me," *To Criticize the Critic* (New York: Farrar, Straus and Giroux, 1965), p. 126.
52. "John Dryden," *Selected Essays*, p. 266.
53. "John Dryden," *The Listener* 3 (April 16, 1930): 688.

unless he enjoys the poetry of Pope as poetry; and I would say the same of Dryden."[54]) Any admirer of eighteenth-century poetry immediately notices the immence advance over the typical nineteenth-century notion of an almost static and absolute realm of "poetry" from which the genre of satire was by its supposed limitations excluded *a priori*. From a valid point of view, satire is merely the *method* that Dryden and Pope used to turn "current life into something rich and strange."[55] In another passage from the essay of 1930 Eliot succeeded in suggesting what one feels to have been the significance of Dryden to his contemporaries, a significance hardly to be comprehended by the term *satire*. Quoting from the lines on Achitophel, he commented, "For my present purpose such verses are only incidentally *satire*. A great poet is a poet who extends the uses of verse; who makes poetry out of what we took for granted to be only matter for prose, written or often only spoken prose. . . . The small poet is the poet who can only use whatever is currently accepted in his time as the poetic material."[56]

It seems to have been these meditations on the significance of Dryden that enabled Eliot in 1950 to formulate the lesson he had drawn from Baudelaire: "that the source of new poetry might be found in what had been regarded hitherto as the impossible, the sterile, the intractably unpoetic. That, in fact, the business of the poet was to make poetry out of the unexplored resources of the unpoetical; that the poet, in fact, was committed by his profession to turn the unpoetical into poetry."[57] One might surmise that these sentences state the "lesson of Eliot," the influence that at their best his poetry and criticism might communicate to the future. From this point of view, it seems just possible to believe that "poetry has always before it, as F.

54. *Ibid.*, p. 689.
55. "London Letter," *The Dial* 71 (August 1921): 214.
56. "John Dryden," *The Listener* 3 (April 16, 1930): 689.
57. "What Dante Means to Me," *To Criticize the Critic*, p. 126.

S. Oliver said of politics, an 'endless adventure.' "[58] The statement of the function of poetry that I have paused to admire might, of course, have a bad influence, encouraging a great deal of dull poetry. But that could happen only if the other half of Eliot's lesson were ignored: "What is needed of art is a simplification of current life into something rich and strange."[59]

We are now ready to examine the function of technique as a method of informing or transforming current life. Returning to "Four Elizabethan Dramatists," let us try, with Eliot, "to conceive how the Elizabethan drama would appear to us if we had in existence what has never existed in the English language: a drama formed within a conventional scheme. . . . It may be some quite new selection or structure or distortion in subject matter or technique; any form or rhythm imposed upon the world of action."[60] This last sentence is not exactly transparent. And it is rather ironic that when we turn to other passages to elucidate it, we find most help in Eliot's earlier remarks on the *virtues* of Elizabethan drama. The key passage for my present purpose is one that demonstrates the relationship between form as self-consistency and form as technique: "The ability to perform that slight distortion of *all* the elements in the world of a play or a story, so that this world is complete in itself, which was given to Marlowe and Jonson (and to Rabelais) and which is prerequisite to great farce, was denied to Massinger."[61] Again we read, "The personages of Tourneur . . . are all distorted to scale."[62] Everywhere during the twenties there are references to forms such as farce, caricature, satire, humor, and to techniques such as simplification, abstraction, intensification, distortion. Inspiration was to be drawn from Marlowe and Jonson, the music hall comedians, Baudelaire. Eliot, his confidence in

---

58. "The Music of Poetry," *On Poetry and Poets*, p. 33.
59. "London Letter," *The Dial* 71 (August 1921): 214.
60. *Selected Essays*, pp. 93–94.
61. "Philip Massinger," *The Sacred Wood*, p. 142, and *Selected Essays*, p. 195.
62. "Cyril Tourneur," *Selected Essays*, p. 162.

imagination as it operated in nineteenth-century English poetry having failed, seems to have desired that the poetry of his generation start from "current life" and that it transform this life by some definite device, some principle almost scientific, even mechanical. His reference to Jonson's "worlds, drawn to scale in every part" even uses a metaphor of the draughtsman's tools.[63]

But if almost mechanical in its operation, this poetic method was not to be trivial or perfunctory. Eliot commented on the "farce" of *The Jew of Malta:* "It is the farce of the old English humour, the terribly serious, even savage comic humour. . . . It is the humour of that very serious (but very different) play, *Volpone.* "[64] Eliot was probably helped to his conception of a peculiarly English humor by a comment of Baudelaire, which he quoted in 1921: "Pour trouver du comique féroce et très-féroce, il faut passer la Manche et visiter les royaumes brumeux du spleen . . . le signe distinctif de ce genre de comique était la violence."[65] In 1921 Eliot wrote that *Volpone* "does not merely show that wickedness is punished; it criticises humanity by intensifying wickedness. How we are reassured about ourselves when we make the acquaintance of such a person on the stage!"[66] This curious remark is illuminated by Eliot's statement, in the essay on Baudelaire almost ten years later, that "the possibility of damnation is so immense a relief in a world of electoral reform, plebiscites, sex reform and dress reform, that damnation itself is an immediate form of salvation."[67]

If we have some difficulty in grasping precisely what Eliot was driving at in this program for his generation set forth in the twenties, I think the reason is fairly simple: the idea

63. "Ben Jonson," *The Sacred Wood,* p. 119, and *Selected Essays,* p. 137.
64. "Notes on the Blank Verse of Christopher Marlowe," *The Sacred Wood,* p. 92, and *Selected Essays,* p. 105.
65. "London Letter," *The Dial* 70 (June 1921): 688.
66. "The Romantic Englishman, the Comic Spirit, and the Function of Criticism," *Tyro* 1 (1922):[4].
67. "Baudelaire," *Selected Essays,* pp. 378–79.

was never realized. Of his own work, only the fragmentary *Sweeney Agonistes* gives some hint of the idea. But we may observe that if Eliot's own remarks are to be respected, at least one English dramatist should have been excepted from the blanket criticism of "Four Elizabethan Dramatists." In that essay he sets against the unlimited realism, the lack of convention, of English drama the example of the ballet: "Any one who has observed one of the great dancers of the Russian school will have observed that the man or the woman whom we admire is a being who exists only during the performances . . . is a conventional being, a being which exists only in and for the work of art which is the ballet."[68] Now this is an application of the same idea Eliot had expressed some years earlier in a comparison of Jonson's method of characterization with that of Shakespeare: "Volpone's life, on the other hand, is bounded by the scene in which it is played; in fact, the life is the life of the scene and is derivatively the life of Volpone; the life of the character is inseparable from the life of the drama."[69] (It is also worth rereading these last two quotations as expressions of the antipersonalism of Eliot's early criticism.) I have already quoted a passage in which Eliot attributed to Jonson's "world" the self-consistency that he later found lacking in Elizabethan drama. That Eliot did not make of Jonson an exception in "Four Elizabethan Dramatists" was perhaps due to a doubt that many of his plays measured up to the standard. But if we keep in mind those great plays *The Alchemist* and *Volpone*, we will have, I think, some insight into the conception of "the theatre, which, if realised, would be the theatre of our generation."[70]

It is not my purpose to canvass systematically Eliot's

68. "Four Elizabethan Dramatists," *Selected Essays*, p. 95.
69. "Ben Jonson," *The Sacred Wood*, p. 112, and *Selected Essays*, pp. 132–133.
70. "Dramatis Personae," *The Criterion* 1 (April 1923): 305.

many remarks on specific techniques. But since I have already quoted his comment on Dryden's powers of turning the prosaic into poetry, it is appropriate to examine briefly what he had to say about the techniques of eighteenth-century poetry. He said surprisingly little about the mock-heroic mode, but we cannot doubt that he was fully aware of its significance as a formal device. In an essay on *Ulysses*, he asserted that "Mr. Joyce's parallel use of the Odyssey has a great importance. It has the importance of a scientific discovery. No one else has built a novel upon such a foundation before. . . . It is because the novel, instead of being a form, was simply the expression of an age which had not sufficiently lost all form to feel the need of something stricter. . . . It is, I seriously believe, a step toward making the modern world possible for art, toward that order and form which Mr. Aldington so earnestly desires."[71] (The distinction in the next to last sentence between form in life and form in art, and the judgment that, as form in life disappears, stricter form in art is required, are elaborated in "A Dialogue on Dramatic Poetry.")

There is abundant evidence of Eliot's interest in the invention, recognition, and refinement of the heroic couplet in the seventeenth and eighteenth centuries.[72] Here is an interesting remark that shows Eliot's insight into the immense power of the perfected couplet as a formal device for turning current life into art: "We do not ordinarily expect a very close structure of a poem in rhymed couplets, which often looks as if, but for what the author has to say, it might begin or end anywhere."[73]

As a way of summarizing the material of this section, I

71. "Ulysses, Order, and Myth," *The Dial* 75 (November 1923): 482–83.

72. See "Sir John Denham," *The Times Literary Supplement* (July 5, 1928), p. 501; "The Minor Metaphysicals: From Cowley to Dryden," *The Listener* 3 (April 9, 1930): 641–42; "Dryden the Dramatist," *The Listener* 5 (April 22, 1931): 681–82; "John Dryden's Tragedies," *The Listener* 29 (April 22, 1943): 486–87.

73. "Johnson as Critic and Poet," *On Poetry and Poets*, pp. 207–8.

record my impression that Eliot had a distinct and, if you wish, peculiar taste in poetry, preferring that in which he could see the poetic transformation in operation, could see at once the material, apparently "intractably unpoetic," the precise operation by which it is transformed, and the product, "rich and strange." In 1951 he remarked, "What I should hope might be achieved, by a generation of dramatists having the benefit of our experience, is that the audience should find, at the moment of awareness that it is hearing poetry, that it is saying to itself: 'I could talk in poetry too!' Then we should not be transported into an artificial world; on the contrary, our own sordid, dreary daily world would be suddenly illuminated and transfigured."[74]

Thus far I have discussed only those aspects of Eliot's concept of form which remain constant throughout all periods of his criticism; I have drawn material indiscriminately from any source without concern for date. But I have already tried to show that that criticism is not to be fully understood without taking account of its chronological development. In a retrospective summary of his critical career, Eliot said, "I find myself constantly irritated by having my words, perhaps written thirty or forty years ago, quoted as if I had uttered them yesterday."[75] Specifically, I have called attention to Eliot's altering attitude toward the concept of the soul and thus toward personality. The development of his critical view in general and of his attitude toward the soul in particular did not take place without development of his concept of form.

74. "Poetry and Drama," *On Poetry and Poets,* p. 87.
75. "To Criticize the Critic," *To Criticize the Critic,* p. 14.

d. Classic Form and Pattern of Development

This development can be approached most simply through an analysis of two distinguishable and contrasting kinds of form that Eliot recognized. One we may call "classic form." It will not do to call the other "romantic form," for though it is not entirely irrelevant, that term would introduce more confusion than illumination. Perhaps the best word for the second kind of form is *pattern*, as in the lines from "Burnt Norton": "Only by the form, the pattern, / Can words or music reach / The stillness." However, since pattern would certainly be a part of classic form as well, it is necessary to add a qualification and thus call the second kind of form "pattern of development."

The essential quality of classic form is stasis. Eliot wrote in 1924:

> A new classical age will be reached when the dogma, or *ideology*, of the critics is so modified by contact with creative writing, and when the creative writers are so permeated by the new dogma, that a state of equilibrium is reached.
>
> For what is meant by a classical moment in literature is surely a moment of *stasis*, when the creative impulse finds a form which satisfies the best intellect of the time, a moment when a type is produced.[76]

In his earliest as in his last essays on Paul Valéry, Eliot drew the same *leçon de Valéry:* "The proper end of the romantic is to achieve the classic," as he wrote in 1947.[77] As he put it in 1924, "Valéry represents . . . the reintegration of the symbolist movement into the great tradition." He indicated the difference between symbolist poetry and that of Valéry this way: "The indefinable difference is the difference between the fluid and the static: between that which

76. "A Commentary," *The Criterion* 2 (April 1924): 232.
77. "Leçon de Valéry," *The Listener* 37 (January 9, 1947): 72.

is moving toward an end and that which knows its end and has reached it; which can afford to stand, changeless, like a statue."[78] I suspect that Eliot's meaning here is much the same as in the following sentence: "When we understand necessity, as Spinoza knew, we are free because we assent."[79]

This last passage but one makes it evident that we are not to understand fully Eliot's concept of form without passing from the level of discursive analysis to that of intuition. Study of the criticism must be completed by study of Eliot's meditations, especially in the *Four Quartets,* on stillness and on movement and on the reconciliation of stillness and movement in the figure of the circle. In fact, the sentence from the 1947 essay on Valéry quoted above was immediately followed by a paraphrase of the last paragraph of the *Four Quartets.*

To say that Eliot's concept of form reaches into "the silence" is not to say that we need attempt at this time to follow him there. What we can do is to recall what is, of course, no secret: the immense debt of the *Four Quartets* to Aristotle's doctrines of potentiality and actuality, of being and becoming, of the unmoved mover and of "that which is only moved and has in it no source of movement." To leaf through the pages of Ross's *Aristotle*—particularly the chapter on the Philosophy of Nature—is to see many of the main ideas of the *Four Quartets* pass in review, and not just the ideas but the very images.[80]

Rather than pursue the intuitive connotations of the word *form,* we may approach form through the concepts

78. "A Brief Introduction to the Method of Paul Valéry," pp. 8–9.
79. "The Perfect Critic," *The Sacred Wood,* p. 11.
80. For example: "The movement of the first heaven is due to the action of God, operating as an object of love and desire. . . . Thus Aristotle is enabled to deduce the existence of the celestial sphere, and to explain its rotation as the nearest approximation possible for a corporeal thing to the eternal unchanging activity of the divine self-knowledge." Sir David Ross, *Aristotle,* pp. 97–98.

explored in this essay by examining Eliot's remarks on the poems of Baudelaire: "Their excellence of form, their perfection of phrasing, and their superficial coherence, may give them the appearance of presenting a definite and final state of mind. In reality, they seem to me to have the external but not the internal form of classic art."[81] Classic form, then, is the expression of "a definite and final state of mind." This formula is equivalent to the description of Valéry's poetry just above. In the essay "What is a Classic?" he described this quality as "maturity."[82] Our earlier examination of the problem of belief and of the connection between individual psychology and the health of society may give rise to some doubt about the possibility of "a definite and final state of mind" under the conditions of modern civilization (as Eliot described them). In fact, in the essay on Baudelaire Eliot recognized that "a poet in a romantic age cannot be a 'classical' poet except in tendency."[83] By 1930 Eliot would seem to have come around, in part and reluctantly, to Hegel's view that the Romantic is the art of the modern world. Indeed, Eliot's comparison of the poetry of Baudelaire and of Gautier is virtually an application, conscious or not, of Hegel's definition of Classic and Romantic art (see chapter 1): "In minor form [Baudelaire] never indeed equalled Théophile Gautier. . . . In the best of the slight verse of Gautier there is a satisfaction, a balance of inwards and form, which we do not find in Baudelaire. He had a greater technical ability than Gautier, and yet the content of feeling is constantly bursting the receptacle."[84]

There is reason to doubt that Eliot himself achieved a definite and final state of mind. As he put it in "East Coker," "One has only learnt to get the better of words /

81. "Baudelaire," *Selected Essays*, p. 375.
82. *On Poetry and Poets*, pp. 54–60 and 62–65.
83. "Baudelaire," *Selected Essays*, p. 376.
84. *Ibid.*, p. 375.

For the thing one no longer has to say." Furthermore, the imperative "fare forward" in the *Four Quartets* and, in criticism, such essays as that of 1940 on Yeats, might suggest that it was not his purpose to achieve such a state.[85] The *leçon de Valéry* has, in fact, two aspects: the negative as well as the positive: "[Valéry] was the most self-conscious of all poets."[86] We have examined some of the difficulties implied, for Eliot, by self-consciousness. It is to be doubted that, unless supported not so much by belief as by *acceptance,* a definite and final state of mind—"that which knows its end and has reached it"—is possible without excessive self-consciousness.

In 1947 Eliot seemed to suggest that Valéry's nihilism— "L'Europe est finie"—was due to his not changing with the

85. It is interesting that the imperative "fare forward" is anticipated by the doctrine of points of view in Eliot's thesis. In chap. 5 we noted that an inherent dilemma of that doctrine is that "we can support a particular point of view" only so long as we do not recognize it as such. It is this implication that still remains to be fully explored. "The point of view (or finite centre) has for its object one consistent world, and accordingly no finite centre can be self-sufficient, for the life of a soul does not consist in the contemplation of one consistent world but in the painful task of unifying (to a greater or less extent) jarring and incompatible ones, and passing, when possible, from two or more discordant viewpoints to a higher which shall somehow include and transmute them." [*Knowledge and Experience,* pp. 147–48]. The "contemplation of one consistent world" which is rejected here would seem to be equivalent to a "definite and final state of mind." For Bradley, there is the Absolute point of view, but Eliot found that to be a matter of faith and not of fact. In 1916 he was able to affirm only that "what we do know is that we are able to pass from one point of view to another, that we are compelled to do so, and that the different aspects more or less hang together." ["Leibniz' Monads and Bradley's Finite Centres," in *Knowledge and Experience,* p. 207]. This would seem to be a demythologized version of Hegel's "dialectic process," its conceptualized stages and its projected "end" removed, leaving an "endless journey to no end." In his later years, Eliot came to accept the idea of progress in certain respects. In 1944 he pointed to "the assumption implicit in all historical study: that we understand the past better than the previous generations did, simply because there is more of it. We assume, and we must assume, a progressive development of consciousness." ["Introduction" to S. L. Bethell, *Shakespeare and the Popular Dramatic Tradition* (Durham, N.C.: Duke University Press, 1945), p. viii.] Another area in which Eliot seems to have assumed a progressive improvement is, surprisingly enough, manners.

86. "From Poe to Valéry," *To Criticize the Critic,* p. 39.

change of Europe: "Valéry's Europe is certainly finished."
What is needed is not Valéry's absolute stasis but change
within a larger pattern of stasis. Compare the following
sentences from "Leçon de Valéry" with the end of the *Four
Quartets:* "The proper end of the romantic is to achieve the
classic—that is to say, every language, to retain its vitality,
must perpetually depart and return upon itself; but without
the departure there is no return and the returning is as
important as the arrival. We have to return to where we
started from, but the journey has altered the starting place:
so that the place we left and the place we return to are the
same and also different."[87]

After 1930 Eliot did not insist on classic form but
stressed another kind. I do not suggest that he altered his
valuation of classic art. Rather I believe that, while up to
about 1930 Eliot saw his critical task as the exposition of his
idea of what his generation ought to achieve, thereafter his
concern was more to recognize, justify and help perfect
what at its best that generation could achieve.

Eliot's observations on the poetry of Baudelaire led to
the conclusion that "the true claim of Baudelaire as an
artist is not that he found a superficial form, but that he was
searching for a form of life."[88] The last three words are not
a careless turn of phrase; they suggest the alternative to
classic form to which I have referred. Applied to poetry
instead of to the poet, the concept would be this: "The
whole of Shakespeare's work is *one* poem."[89]

Virgil and Dante were for Eliot the great poets of classic
form; of the other kind of form the perfection is the work
of Shakespeare.

87. "Leçon de Valéry," *The Listener* 37 (January 9, 1947): 72.
88. "Baudelaire," *Selected Essays*, p. 375.
89. "John Ford," *Selected Essays*, p. 179.

The standard set by Shakespeare is that of a continuous development from first to last, a development in which the choice
both of theme and of dramatic and verse technique in each play
seems to be determined increasingly by Shakespeare's state of
feeling, by the particular stage of his emotional maturity at the
time. What is "the whole man" is not simply his greatest or
maturest achievement, but the whole pattern formed by the
sequence of plays; so that we may say confidently that the full
meaning of any one of his plays is not in itself alone, but in that
play in the order in which it was written, in its relation to all
of Shakespeare's other plays, earlier and later: we must know
all of Shakespeare's work in order to know any of it. No other
dramatist of the time approaches anywhere near to this perfection of pattern, of pattern superficial and profound.[90]

This second concept of form seems to involve more reference to the poet than would have been approved in the
early criticism. I suggested in the previous chapter that
Eliot's changed attitude toward the soul did alter his attitude toward personality, though within certain limits; the
change does not affect the *poet:* his aim must remain "to see
the object as in itself it really is." The *reader,* however, is
allowed to look through the poetry at the poet: the latter
is apparently not entirely insubstantial.

In 1940 Eliot offered some observations on the place of
personality in poetry which I suspect are meant to be compared, almost phrase by phrase, with the valuations of
"Tradition and the Individual Talent." Explaining his view
that Yeats developed from a great craftsman, in his early
works, into a great poet, in his later, Eliot wrote:

In any anthology, you find some poems which give you complete satisfaction and delight in themselves, such that you are
hardly curious who wrote them, hardly want to look further
into the work of that poet. There are others, not necessarily so
perfect or complete, which make you irresistibly curious to
know more of that poet through his other work. . . . Now

90. *Ibid.,* p. 170.

among all of the poems in Yeats's earlier volumes I find only
in a line here or there, that sense of a unique personality which
makes one sit up in excitement and eagerness to learn more
about the author's mind and feelings.[91]

A critical view based on the concept of the objective
correlative always has implicit in it the possibility of a symbolic interpretation of art; in any idealist theory it is impossible to deny absolutely the tendency of the poem to be
referred to the poet. In his early criticism Eliot resisted this
tendency to the point of pushing idealism to—or over—the
verge of behaviorism: "the dramatist need not understand
people; but he must be exceptionally aware of them."[92] But
by 1932, Eliot was suggesting that "a dramatic poet cannot
create characters of the greatest intensity of life unless his
personages, in their reciprocal actions and behaviour in
their story, are somehow dramatizing, but in no obvious
form, an action or struggle for harmony in the soul of the
poet."[93]

Eliot even came to refer to this deeper pattern—"as it
would often be called, personality"—as "the essential" as
against the "superficies."[94] Ford and Beaumont and
Fletcher imitated Shakespeare's devices, such as the Recognition Scene, but "they had no conception of what he was
trying to do. . . . In their poetry there is no symbolic value;
theirs is good poetry and good drama, but it is poetry and
drama of the surface."[95] With Eliot, however, no change is
ever absolute, and so we are reminded that "in a work of
art, as truly as anywhere, reality only exists in and through
appearances. . . . Poetry is poetry, and the surface is as
marvellous as the core." This qualification was made in
Eliot's introduction to G. W. Knight's *The Wheel of Fire*,

91. "Yeats," *On Poetry and Poets*, pp. 298–99.
92. "Philip Massinger," *The Sacred Wood*, p. 132, and *Selected Essays*, p. 188.
93. "John Ford," *Selected Essays*, pp. 172–73.
94. "Thomas Heywood," *Selected Essays*, p. 153.
95. "John Ford," *Selected Essays*, p. 172.

where Eliot first publicly accepted the necessity of "interpretation."[96]

It would certainly be wrong to suggest that Eliot moved in his later criticism from "the Impersonal theory of poetry" to a biographical approach. But that is in part because in the great poets "there is the essential, as well as the superficies, of poetry; they give the pattern, or we may say the undertone, of the personal emotion, the personal drama and struggle, *which no biography, however full and intimate, could give us.*"[97] There is one more fact to be accounted for, one that may seem at first rather odd: Eliot pointed over and over again to the existence of a pattern in the work of Shakespeare, but he nowhere offered a specific interpretation of that pattern. On reflection, we realize that this fact is not odd but entirely characteristic of the critic and entirely true to the principles of his criticism: "I suspect, in fact, that a good deal of the value of an interpretation is—that it should be my own interpretation."[98]

96. (London: Oxford University Press, 1930), p. xx.
97. "John Ford," *Selected Essays,* p. 180. (Emphasis mine.)
98. "The Frontiers of Criticism," *On Poetry and Poets,* p. 127.

Conclusion

"We should begin to learn to distinguish the appreciation of poetry from theorising about poetry, and to know when we are not talking about poetry but about something else suggested by it."[1] The analysis of knowledge and experience that Eliot had made in his thesis left him acutely aware of how small a fraction of the total time we devote to a poem is given up to direct appreciation—immediate experience—of it; and aware also that in comparison to those moments of direct appreciation all else is the shadow of a shade; and aware, finally, of how easy it is, in the study of poetry, to be tempted from direct experience to reflection. The severity of Eliot's comments on those kinds of criticism he believed to be beside the point is a consequence of this awareness, and another consequence, perhaps, was occasional doubt as to the use of criticism at all. The reserve of his critical style is precisely a tribute to the irreplaceability of our own experience of the poem.

But this is not all there is to be said about criticism, for "the experience of a poem is the experience both of a moment and of a lifetime."[2] In 1920 Eliot observed that "even a quite uninitiated reader" might have a powerful initial experience of the *Divine Comedy*, "an impression of

1. *The Use of Poetry*, 2nd ed. (London: Faber and Faber, 1964), p. 123.
2. "Dante," *Selected Essays*, 2nd ed. (New York: Harcourt, Brace and World, 1960), p. 212.

171

overpowering beauty. . . . This impression may be so deep that no subsequent study and understanding will intensify it." To have stopped here would have been for him to occupy the position of the critical impressionist—and undoubtedly there was a genuine impulse toward anti-intellectualism in Eliot. However, he continued immediately, "But at this point the impression is emotional; the reader in the ignorance which we postulate is unable to distinguish the poetry from an emotional state aroused in himself by the poetry, a state which may be merely an indulgence of his own emotions." And so he went on to protest "the torpid superstition that appreciation is one thing, and 'intellectual' criticism something else."[3]

But the ultimate justification of criticism is not that it is useful, but that it is "inevitable." Here Eliot appropriated the wry humor of Bradley: "Criticism may be, what F. H. Bradley said of metaphysics, 'the finding of bad reasons for what we believe upon instinct, but to find these reasons is no less an instinct.' "[4] Therefore, accepting what is both useful and inevitable, the critic may proceed with a clear conscience, with the one proviso that "his end . . . be the return to the work of art with improved perception and intensified, because more conscious, enjoyment."[5]

Eliot's critical thought continues the Romantic tradition, at least in the sense that his fundamental critical concepts originate in idealist epistemology. More specifically, Eliot's critical theory is remarkably Hegelian. (Of course, the influence of Hegel would be mostly indirect, through Bradley.) I say "remarkably," because Eliot's occasional comments on Hegel are at best not complimentary. But I do not suggest that Eliot's strictures on Hegel are insincere. To a

3. "The Perfect Critic," *The Sacred Wood*, 2nd ed. (London: Methuen, 1960), pp. 14–15.

4. "To Criticize the Critic," *To Criticize the Critic* (New York: Farrar, Straus and Giroux, 1965), p. 11.

5. "The Perfect Critic," *The Sacred Wood*, p. 13.

reader who raised some questions about "The Perfect
Critic," Eliot replied that "Hegel's 'Philosophy of Art' adds
very little to our enjoyment or understanding of art, though
it fills a gap in Hegel's philosophy."[6] Eliot's view of the
function of criticism certainly differed from that which he
imputed to Hegel; he was objecting here to that tendency
to subjectivism which he found characteristic of the Romantic tradition.

Eliot's conception of the role of personality, whether in
the composition or in the criticism of poetry, reveals both
his fundamental agreement with and his reaction against
Romanticism. As to the *fact* of the inescapable subjectivity
of human experience, Eliot agrees with the Romantic critics, but in his *attitude* to this fact he differs sharply. To Remy
de Gourmont, the doctrine that "the world is my representation" was "the universal principle of emancipation for all
men capable of comprehending." To Eliot, subjectivity is
a terrible limitation, to transcend which the effort of a
whole lifetime is not too great a price, even though that
effort can never succeed. But Eliot did not abandon the
Romantic premise. For him, the poet's or the critic's expression of his personality in his work may be a sin, but it
is original sin.

We may say, then, that if Eliot's critical theory is in the
Romantic tradition, his critical practice is *an effort to escape
from that theory.* One can conceive of at least two possible
ways of escape from theory: one would be to embody the
theory in a system of concrete critical judgements; the
other would be to succeed in seeing the object as in itself
it really is. No doubt Eliot's aim was to take the second way.
But since that would be an end never to be fully realized,
we may say that Eliot's critical practice falls somewhere
between these two relations to theory.

6. "The Perfect Critic: To the Editor of *The Athenaeum*," *The Athenaeum* (August
6, 1920), p. 190.

In his early criticism Eliot seems to have tried to confront directly the problems raised by nineteenth-century aesthetics and sociology, whether to destroy or to fulfill is not quite certain. And I think the final result of this confrontation is uncertain, too. It is my opinion that, if Eliot succeeded in advancing beyond nineteenth-century criticism, it was not so much by solving the problems it had raised as by supplementing its profundity with the sanity of earlier criticism. As he wrote in 1929,

> "For the earlier period, art and literature were not substitutes for religion or philosophy or morals or politics, any more than for duelling or love-making: they were special and limited adornments of life. On each side there is a profit and a loss. We have gained perhaps a deeper insight, now and then; whether we enjoy literature any more keenly than our ancestors I do not know; but I think we should return again and again to the critical writings of the seventeenth and eighteenth centuries, to remind ourselves of that simple truth that literature is primarily literature, a means of refined and intellectual pleasure.[7]

In other words, we ought to consider our examination of Eliot's theoretical writings as merely a preface to what, in "To Criticize the Critic," he said he wished to be remembered for: his appreciations of individual authors. To pursue that topic, however, we should turn directly to the writings of Eliot.

7. "Experiment in Criticism," *The Bookman* 70 (November 1929): 227.

Selected Bibliography

Aristotle. *The Works of Aristotle.* Edited by W. D. Ross. 12 vols. Oxford: Oxford University Press, 1908–52.

———. *The Poetics,* in *Classical Literary Criticism.* Translated by T. S. Dorsch. Baltimore: Penguin Books, 1965.

Arnold, Matthew. *Culture and Anarchy.* Edited by J. Dover Wilson. Cambridge, England: Cambridge University Press, 1960 [a reprint of the edition of 1932].

———. *Essays in Criticism.* 2nd ed. New York: Dutton, 1964.

Babbitt, Irving. *Rousseau and Romanticism.* Cleveland: The World Publishing Company, 1955 [a reprint of the edition of 1919].

Bradley, Francis Herbert. *Appearance and Reality.* 2nd ed. Oxford: Clarendon Press, 1930.

———. *Collected Essays.* 2 vols. Oxford: Clarendon Press, 1935.

———. *Essays on Truth and Reality.* Oxford: Clarendon Press, 1914.

———. *The Principles of Logic.* 2nd ed. 2 vols. London: Oxford University Press, 1922.

Coleridge, Samuel T. *Selected Poetry and Prose of Coleridge.* Edited by Donald A. Stauffer. New York: Random House, 1951.

Copleston, Frederick. *A History of Philosophy.* rev. ed. 8 vols. Garden City, N. Y.: Doubleday and Company, 1962–1967.

Damon, Samuel Foster. *Amy Lowell.* New York and Boston: Houghton Mifflin Company, 1935.

DeLaura, David J. "Pater and Eliot: The Origin of the 'Objective Correlative,'" *Modern Language Quarterly* 26 (1965): 426–31.

Dewey, John. "Reality and the Criterion for the Truth of Ideas," *Mind* n.s.16 (July 1907): 317–42.

Dryden, John. *Of Dramatic Poesy and Other Critical Essays.* Edited by

George Watson. 2 vols. New York: E. P. Dutton and Company, 1964.

Eliot, T. S. *After Stange Gods*. New York: Harcourt, Brace and Company, 1934.

———. "Andrew Marvell," *The Nation & The Athenaeum* 33 (September 29, 1923): 809.

———. "The Beating of a Drum," *The Nation & The Athenaeum* 34 (October 6, 1923): 11–12.

———. "A Brief Introduction to the Method of Paul Valéry," in *Paul Valéry, Le Serpent*. Translated by Mark Wardle. London: R. Cobden-Sanderson, 1924.

———. "A Commentary," *The Criterion* 2 (April 1924): 231–35.

———. "A Commentary," *The Criterion* 12 (April 1933): 468–73.

———. "A Commentary: That Poetry Is Made with Words," *The New English Weekly* 15 (April 27, 1939): 27–28.

———. *The Complete Poems and Plays, 1909–1950*. New York: Harcourt, Brace and World, 1962.

———. "Deux Attitudes Mystiques," *Le Roseau D'Or* 14 (1927): 149–73.

———. "The Development of Leibniz' Monadism," *The Monist* 26 (October 1916): 534–56: reprinted as "Appendix I" of *Knowledge and Experience*, pp. 177–97.

———. "Donne in Our Time," in *A Garland for John Donne*. Edited by Theodore Spencer. Cambridge, Mass.: Harvard University Press, 1931.

———. "Dramatis Personae," *The Criterion* 1 (April 1923): 303–6.

———. "Dryden the Critic, Defender of Sanity," *The Listener* 5 (April 29, 1931): 724–25.

———. "Dryden the Dramatist," *The Listener* 5 (April 22, 1931): 681–82.

———. "The Education of Taste," *The Athenaeum* (June 27, 1919), pp. 520–21.

———. "Eeldrop and Appleplex, I," *The Little Review* 4 (May 1917): 7–11.

———. "Experiment in Criticism," *The Bookman* 70 (November 1929): 225–33.

———. "The Function of a Literary Review," *The Criterion* 1 (July 1923): 421.

———. "[A review of] *The Growth of Civilization* and *The Origin of Magic*," by W. J. Perry. *The Criterion* 2 (July 1924): 489–91.

———. *The Idea of a Christian Society,* in *Christianity and Culture.* New York: Harcourt, Brace and Company, 1949.

———. "In Memory," *The Little Review* 5 (August 1918): 44–47.

———. "Introduction" to S. L. Bethell, *Shakespeare and the Popular Dramatic Tradition.* Durham, N.C.: Duke University Press, 1945.

———. "Introduction" to G. Wilson Knight, *The Wheel of Fire.* London: Oxford University Press, 1930.

———. "Isolated Superiority," *The Dial* 84 (January 1928): [4]–7.

———. "John Donne," *The Nation & The Athenaeum* 33 (June 9, 1923): 331–32.

———. "John Dryden," *The Listener* 3 (April 16, 1930): 688–89.

———. "John Dryden's Tragedies," *The Listener* 29 (April 22, 1943): 486–87.

———. "Kipling Redivivus," *The Athenaeum* (May 9, 1919), pp. 297–98.

———. *Knowledge and Experience in the Philosophy of F. H. Bradley.* New York: Farrar, Straus and Company, 1964.

———. "Leçon de Valéry," *The Listener* 37 (January 9, 1947): 72.

———. "Leibniz' Monads and Bradley's Finite Centres," *The Monist* 26 (October 1916): 566–76: reprinted as "Appendix II" of *Knowledge and Experience,* pp. 198–207.

———. "London Letter," *The Dial* 70 (June 1921): [686]–691.

———. "London Letter," *The Dial* 71 (August 1921): [213]–217.

———. "London Letter," *The Dial* 72 (May 1922): [510]–513.

———. "The Minor Metaphysicals: From Cowley to Dryden." *The Listener* 3 (April 9, 1930): 641–42.

———. "The Mysticism of Blake." *The Nation & The Athenaeum* 41 (September 17, 1927): 779.

———. "[A review of] *The Name and Nature of Poetry." The Criterion* 13 (October 1933): 151–54.

———. "The Need for Poetic Drama." *The Listener* 16 (November 25, 1936): 994–95.

———. "Nicolo Machiavelli." *The Times Literary Supplement,* June 16, 1927, pp. [413]–414.

———. "Notes on the Way," *Time and Tide* 16 (January 5, 1935): 6–[7].

———. "Notes on the Way," *Time and Tide* 16 (January 19, 1935): 88–90.

———. *Notes towards the Definition of Culture.* In *Christianity and Culture.* New York: Harcourt, Brace and Company, 1949.

————. *On Poetry and Poets.* New York: Farrar, Straus and Giroux, 1961.

————. "The Poetic Drama." *The Athenaeum* (May 14, 1920), pp. 635–36.

————. "The Preacher as Artist," *The Athenaeum* (November 28, 1919), pp. 1252–53.

————. "A Preface to Modern Literature," *Vanity Fair* 21 (November 1923): 44 and 118.

————. "Reflections on Contemporary Poetry," *The Egoist* 6 (July 1919): 39–40.

————. "Reflections on Contemporary Poetry," *The Egoist* 4 (October 1917): 133–34.

————. "[A review of] *Religion and Science*" by John Theodore Merz. *International Journal of Ethics* 27 (October 1916): 125–26.

————. "Religion without Humanism." In *Humanism and America,* edited by Norman Foerster. New York: Farrar and Rinehart, 1930.

————. "Rhyme and Reason: The Poetry of John Donne." *The Listener* 3 (March 19, 1930): 502–3.

————. "The Romantic Englishman, the Comic Spirit, and the Function of Criticism," *Tyro* 1 (1922): [4].

————. *The Sacred Wood.* 2nd ed. London: Methuen, 1960 [a reprint of the edition of 1928].

————. *Selected Essays.* 2nd ed. New York: Harcourt, Brace and World, 1960.

————. "Sir John Denham." *The Times Literary Supplement,* July 5, 1928, p. 501.

————. "Studies in Contemporary Criticism," *The Egoist* 5 (October 1918): [113]–114.

————. "T. S. Eliot: The Art of Poetry" [an interview], *The Paris Review* 21 (Spring/Summer 1959): 47–70.

————. *To Criticize the Critic.* New York: Farrar, Straus and Giroux, 1965.

————. "Ulysses, Order, and Myth," *The Dial* 75 (November 1923): [480]–483.

————. *The Use of Poetry and the Use of Criticism.* 2nd ed. London: Faber and Faber, 1964.

————. "Views and Reviews." *The New English Weekly* 7 (June 20, 1935): 190–91.

―――. "War-Paint and Feathers," *The Athenaeum* (October 17, 1919), p. 1036.

Gay, Peter. *The Enlightenment.* New York: Alfred A. Knopf, 1966.

Geertz, Clifford. "In Search of North Africa." *The New York Review of Books* 16 (April 22, 1971): 20–24.

Gourmont, Remy de. *Selected Writings.* Translated and edited by Glenn S. Burne. Ann Arbor: University of Michigan Press, 1966.

Harding, D. W. "The Eyes Have It." *The New York Review of Books* 16 (April 22, 1971): 39–41.

Hegel, Georg Wilhelm Friedrich. *The Philosophy of Hegel.* Edited by Carl J. Friedrich. New York: Random House, 1953.

Manser, A. B. "Imagination." *The Encyclopedia of Philosophy.* 1967. 4:136–38.

Maurron, Charles. "Concerning 'Intuition.'" *The Criterion* 6 (September 1927): 229–35.

Miller, Joseph Hillis. *Poets of Reality.* Cambridge, Mass.: Harvard University Press, 1965.

Pater, Walter. *The Renaissance.* Introduction by Kenneth Clark. Cleveland: The World Publishing Company, 1961.

Plato. *The Collected Dialogues of Plato.* Edited by Edith Hamilton and Huntington Cairns. New York: Bollingen Foundation, 1963.

Ross, Sir David. *Aristotle.* 5th ed. London: Methuen, 1964.

Runes, Dagobert D., ed. *Dictionary of Philosophy.* Ames, Iowa: Littlefield, Adams and Company, 1955.

Russell, Bertrand. *A History of Western Philosophy.* New York: Simon and Schuster, 1945.

―――. *My Philosophical Development.* New York: Simon and Schuster, 1959.

Soldo, John J. "Knowledge and Experience in the Criticism of T. S. Eliot." *A Journal of English Literary History* 35 (June 1968): 284–308.

Symons, Arthur. *The Symbolist Movement in Literature.* rev. ed. Introduction by Richard Ellmann. New York: E. P. Dutton and Company, 1958.

Taylor, A. E. [A review of] *Idola Theatri, a Criticism of Oxford Thought and Thinkers,* by Henry Sturt. *Mind* 22, n.s.16 (July 1907): 424–30.

Urmson, J. O. "Ideas," *The Encyclopedia of Philosophy.* 1967. 4: 118–21.

Warren, Henry Clarke, trans. and ed. *Buddhism in Translations.* New York: Atheneum, 1963.

White, Alan R. "Coherence Theory of Truth," *The Encyclopedia of Philosophy.* 1967. 2:130–33.

Whiteside, George. "T. S. Eliot's Dissertation." *A Journal of English Literary History* 34 (September 1967): 400–424.

Wollheim, Richard. "Eliot and F. H. Bradley: An Account." In *Eliot in Perspective: A Symposium,* ed. Graham Martin. New York: Humanities Press, 1970.

———. "Eliot, Bradley and Immediate Experience," *New Statesman* 67 (March 13, 1964): 401–2.

———. *F. H. Bradley.* 2nd ed. Baltimore: Penguin Books, 1969.

Yeats, William Butler. *The Autobiography of William Butler Yeats.* New York: The Macmillan Company, 1965.

Index

181

One of the central problems of criticism has always been to define the degree to which literature should reflect the external world and the degree to which it should express the personality of the writer. It is no accident, then, that since Coleridge English criticism has been closely involved with idealist epistemology, which raises just those questions about perception in general. T. S. Eliot's fundamental critical concepts originated in his study of F. H. Bradley's version of the idealist theory of knowledge. But for Eliot, as for Bradley, the great weakness of the Romantic-idealist tradition was its tendency to subjectivism. The destructive criticism of personality in Eliot's early criticism corresponds to Bradley's denial that the individual self or soul is ultimately real and, like it, is directed against the subjective idealism ("The world is my idea") of writers such as Nietzsche, Schopenhauer, and Pater.

This subjectivism Eliot saw as a late stage of a "fearful progress in self-consciousness" in Western culture, the first hints of which can be seen in Shakespeare and his contemporaries. The main theme of Eliot's dissertation on Bradley is a destructive criticism of the psychological